EARLY PRAISE FOR MICHAEL BERVELL'S UNLOCKING UNICORNS

"Michael has crafted a unique, must-read collection of stories from startup founders around the world. Backed by interviews and relatable stories, it's like How I Built This by Guy Raz, but with even more diverse founders, nuanced findings, and evidence-based business advice."

— RACHEL GREENWALD, NEW YORK TIMES BEST SELLING

AUTHOR, FOUNDER & CEO OF ELEVATED CONNECTIONS

"Michael's eloquent writing uncovers truly new insight and gives actionable steps that every investor, operator, and founder can incorporate to level up their work."

— JESSICA LI, VENTURE PARTNER AT PREDICTIVE VC

"*Everyone should read Unlocking Unicorns to learn from some of the most disruptive entrepreneurs making an impact on a global scale. Michael has uncovered the backstories of international legends. It's a must-read for aspiring entrepreneurs and investors interested in the next unicorn.*"

— AYUSHI SINHA, CO-FOUNDER OF PROSPECT
STUDENT VENTURES, PRINCETON'S FIRST
STUDENT-LED VENTURE CAPITAL FUND

"*Refreshing. Motivating. And, for the diaspora, empowering.*"

— MUTESA SITHOLE, GLOBAL CONTENT LEAD AT
INFOBIP (CROATIA'S FIRST TECH UNICORN)

"*One of the joys of reading is to discover unheard stories: Michael reveals real treasures on every page. Travel is one way to experience new cultures, ideas, and perspectives; reading is the next best thing. Through Unlocking Unicorns, you can't help but see the way the world works in ways you've probably never thought of before.*"

— PATRICK LYONS, FOUNDER & CEO OF THE
LYON SHRED AND THE ONLINE COACH ACADEMY,
MECHANICAL SOURCING ENGINEER AT MICROSOFT

UNLOCKING
UNICORNS

Grace!!

Thank you so much
for your support 😊
I hope you enjoy
the stories in
this book!! #NERDLab

Michael Berrell

UNLOCKING UNICORNS

TEN STARTUP STORIES FROM DIVERSE BILLION-DOLLAR FOUNDERS IN AFRICA, ASIA, AND THE MIDDLE EAST

MICHAEL BERVELL

UNLOCKING UNICORNS
Ten Startup Stories from Diverse Billion-dollar Founders in Africa, Asia, and the Middle East

ISBN   978-1-63730-326-9 *Paperback*
           978-1-63730-327-6 *Kindle Ebook*
           978-1-63730-328-3 *Ebook*

Dedication

*This book is dedicated to the more than 750,000
readers, viewers, subscribers, and unsubscribers
of my blog, BillionDollarStartupIdeas.com*

*Your eyeballs and comments inspired me to write every
day for more than 600 days. Thank you for following
my creative journey and giving me the confidence to
publish my digital thoughts in a physical form.*

CONTENTS

———

INTRODUCTION

———

Elias Torres carried a backpack with him when he first moved to the United States. With his jet-black hair and silver wire-rimmed glasses, Elias looked just like every other Nicaraguan immigrant looking to escape a civil war.

But he was different.

His backpack contained a few of his prized possessions: a brochure from the University of California about "computer science" and photos of his wheelchair-bound father. Smiling and full of energy, Elias emigrated to Florida with his mother and two younger brothers. Despite being only seventeen, Elias was "the man of the house." He balanced being a high school student in a country where he didn't know the language with working full-time at two jobs to support his family. Elias' eyes soften as he tells me about his career growth:

My aunt got me and my mother a job cleaning office spaces at night. Then I applied for a McDonald's job and started working there early on. At McDonald's, I was getting paid

$4.75 an hour: that was the minimum wage at the time. Then I got a raise for a dime. My mentality at that moment and for the next following years was that everything in my life was an hourly wage. It started at $4.75, then $4.85, then I went to Albertsons $5.10, then I went to Bank of America and it was $6.25, and the second year of the internship it was $7.25. Finally, I got a job at IBM, and it was like $15 an hour. At the time, it just blew my mind.[1]

He laughs in retrospect. Calculating his net worth in hours now would blow his whole family's mind.

Elias had hustle: he was constantly rubbing two quarters together to make a dollar. After studying business at the University of South Florida, his fire helped him to explode forward: becoming a technical lead for IBM's CIO Office Innovation Team; obtaining a Master's in Computer Science from Harvard; and creating his first company Performable, which he eventually sold to HubSpot for $20 million.[2]

Today, Elias runs Drift. It's a conversational marketing and sales platform that has over 150,000 business customers and is one of the fastest-growing SaaS companies of all time. In July 2020, Elias' company was valued at over $360 million. Not bad, for a child escaping a civil war.

Due to generational wealth, Elias' children will never need to experience the struggles that their father did. By all measures, Elias' story is a great example of the American Dream; an immigrant who came from nothing, started working at McDonalds, and now has enough money to buy the store that used to employ him. It's rags to riches.

This book is not about the American Dream.

While it features rags to riches stories about individuals who have created "Unicorn Companies" (companies valued at $1 billion or more), it is not even about America.

According to the State Department, only 43 percent of Americans have a passport. That figure is increasing at merely 2-3 percent per year. While the whole purpose of the American Dream is for immigrants to breed innovation on American soil, less than half of all Americans want to be an immigrant themselves, even if only to travel for vacation. The flip side of the American Dream is overindulged American exceptionalism: expecting and believing that the United States has the best startups, the best ideas, and the best conditions for innovation globally.

This is simply not true.

Over the last decade, the percentage of Chinese internet users as a share of population has more than doubled, rising from 22.6 percent in 2008 to 59.6 percent in 2018. That accounts for 792 million people: more than twice the population of the United States and twenty times the population of Canada. This makes China the world leader of internet users.

It's not just China that is outpacing American growth. India is one of the largest and fastest-growing markets for digital consumers, with 560 million internet subscribers in 2018, second only to China.[3] This growth is true on the continent of Africa as well. In the past month, more people in Africa accessed the internet than did people in Latin America,

North America, or the Middle East.[4] There were 525 million internet users in Africa, 447 million in Latin America and the Caribbean, 328 million in North America, and 174 million in the Middle East.[5]

The world is changing. It's magnitudes larger than "The American Dream." While innovation can come from anywhere and the United States will continue to produce successful entrepreneurs like Elias Torres, learning the stories of non-American entrepreneurs who have seen success in Africa, the Middle East, and Asia is imperative to understanding tomorrow's innovation. Building the billion-dollar companies of the future will require an intimate understanding of the next billion users.

I realized this firsthand while meeting with Asian technology executives at the World Internet Conference in 2017. As one of four American college-aged delegates selected to attend, I was able to sit down over meals with technology executives like Jack Ma (Alibaba), Robin Li (Baidu), and Ren Zhengfei (Huawei). I probably met more billionaires during that four-day conference than most people see their whole lives.

What struck me in these conversations was that ideas, while valuable, are infinite. What sets successful entrepreneurs apart from unsuccessful ones is execution. This book is the key to learning the habits of execution from the rare outliers in emerging markets who have done it already before. It focuses on the untold stories that you won't hear in traditional American business literature to provide insights for building successful startups that transcend traditional, Western business school canon.

Currently I work as a venture capitalist at Microsoft where my job is literally to give people millions of dollars to build their ideas. Hearing hundreds of pitches, seeing thousands of businesses, conducting due diligence on million-dollar deals, and working directly with CXO entrepreneurs have taught me one thing: anyone can make a startup and be successful if they unlock the habits of Unicorn founders.

Whether you are hoping to build a profitable company, want to learn about what the world will be like in ten years, or are just interested in international business, these stories will open your eyes to the world. How did a brewmaster become the first self-made Indian female billionaire (Chapter 2)? How did one Asian entrepreneur invent Google before Larry Page (Chapter 7)? How did an Indian entrepreneur build a hotel company the size of Marriott in 7.5 percent of the time (Chapter 8)?

These stories and others have been translated to English and packaged for you.

Over the last nine months, I embarked on a journey to directly interview successful billion-dollar founders from Africa, Asia, and the Middle East. While I was able to talk with many of these executives directly, in cases where I was not granted an interview, I adopted a strategy of secondary interviews. This tactic (which I learned while conducting independent research with Jill Abramson, the first female executive editor of the *New York Times*) required that I listen to hundreds of hours of podcasts, direct interviews, keynote speeches, panel discussions, and team meetings to recreate the archetype of the ten founders profiled in this book. I traced digital breadcrumbs to recreate the pie. After all, what would these founders tell me in a one-hour meeting that I couldn't learn through watching more than forty hours of their already available public interviews?

Organized into three parts, this book reflects the three phases that African, Asian, and Middle Eastern unicorn entrepreneurs traverse to create their companies. Phase one is *exploration* to discover an idea worth pursuing (Chapters 1-3), phase two is *refinement* of this idea into a business (Chapters 4-7), and phase three is *execution* to scale (Chapters 8-10). In studying the ten entrepreneurs profiled in this book, you will develop a lens of clarity about how these ten archetypes and personalities have navigated the three phases to develop a combined $10+ trillion in global economic value.

Forget about the American Dream. Instead, Unlock Unicorns.

PART 1:

EXPLORATION

"Life is either a daring adventure or nothing at all."

—HELEN KELLER

In college, I carried around Moleskin® notebooks with me everywhere I went. They were about the size of a credit card and as thick as two cracked iPhone Xs. I prided myself on buying pants with pockets to wrap my written thoughts snuggly alongside my engraved pen. Each notebook was two hundred blank pages. Lines would have been too restricting. Each varied in colors: black (freshman year), green (sophomore year), red (junior year), and yellow (senior year).

These notebooks were my brain on a page as I journeyed through Harvard.

Every semester I would choose a different prompt to inspire me to write daily:

- Freshman fall I recorded every dream I had.
- Freshman spring was a record of the life stories of every peer I had lunch with.
- Sophomore fall I found problems worth solving in the world.
- Sophomore spring my Moleskin® became a poker notebook: defining terms, recording wins, analyzing losses, developing betting strategies, and understanding the percentage-to-win ratios for different hands.
- Junior fall I learned one new vocabulary word every day.
- Junior spring I ideated on ways to optimize restaurant marketing in Harvard square.
- Senior fall I wrote one poem a day.
- Senior spring I started writing one business idea every day.

I always noticed a trend with these books: the first fourteen days were always the most difficult. Getting over the hump of writing *something* around a specific topic every day was a difficult task. I was forced to look for inspiration everywhere. The over-ripe banana in the dining hall became a poem on the decomposition of the human experience, and every class about Aristotle's Nicomachean Ethics caused me to question if poker really was the "good life." Every interaction was colored by the notebook of the moment.

After about one hundred days of carrying each notebook, its color would change: worn down by the use, friction, or the weight of ideas. Those notebooks have seen drunk nights and date nights, washing machines and walking tours, networking calls and not-so-successful interview interrogations. They viewed my life in black and white: as objective as a camera's lens and as private as the homunculi in my head.

> *"A ship in harbor is safe, but that is not what ships are built for."*
>
> —JOHN A. SHEDD

While all founders must embark on similar journeys to expand their world views before creating companies, the three founders you'll read about in Part 1 are exceptional embodiments of exploration. They started by either intentionally or unintentionally exploring the world around them, and even as Unicorn company CEOs, continue to use their unique skills to succeed.

First is Jack Ma, the founder of Alibaba who has more than 1,001 failures. Jack's involuntary exploration through failure forced him to develop *Guanxi* and enabled him to strategically use his networks to grow Alibaba from an idea to an icon in the Chinese market.

Second is Kiran Mazumdar-Shaw, the failed medical school student who is now the *only* self-made female billionaire in India. Through-and-through, she is a contrarian who found business success by exploring and exploiting the realms of what was possible in a male-dominated India.

Third is Mitchell Elegbe, the founder of Interswitch, a Nigerian payments company valued at more than $1 billion and the first African-founded FinTech unicorn company on the continent. More than aimlessly exploring, Mitchell embraced hindsight, foresight, and insight to capitalize on Nigeria's movement toward a cashless economy.

> *"Only those who risk going too far can possibly find out how far one can go."*
>
> —T.S. ELIOT

While none of these three individuals may have carried around a Moleskin® notebook with business ideas or poetry, each has exhibited in his or her own way the importance of exploring the world before starting and while running their Unicorn companies.

Chapter Summary

Lesson 1. At the end of each chapter, you'll find a chapter summary section that looks like this.

Lesson 2. Each chapter summary will pull out the three key lessons of the chapter.

Lesson 3. If you're interested in learning the main lessons of a chapter before reading it, skim this section at the end of each chapter for a quick summary.

CHAPTER 1:

1,001 FAILURES

———

Jack Ma is a failure.

He's a former English teacher; co-founder of the Alibaba Group; and according to Forbes, he's the richest man in China. Founded in 1999, Alibaba, his company, boasts 960 million annual active customers (twice the combined populations of the United States, Canada, and Mexico); 86,000 employees; and $60 billion in annual revenue.[6] But, despite conventional measures of success, even Jack describes himself as a mistake-ridden failure.[7]

We have made thousands of mistakes! Jack says with glee. As an entrepreneur, I don't try to learn from other people about how they succeed, I try to learn from how people fail.[8]

He leaned in and gestured for me to do the same:

I remember some business school came to Alibaba to write a case study. After a one-week study they wanted me to sign the case study. They said, "This is Alibaba."

I read it and responded, "This is not Alibaba! I know this is not me."

They said, "Jack. You don't know you. This case study is Alibaba."

"Well...Alright, fine".[9]

Every year for the next five years, Jack was invited to sit in the back of the classroom to listen as the case study was taught in Tsinghua University. In each case study, the facts pitted Alibaba against competitors and students always unanimously agreed that Alibaba would die. However, five years later, Alibaba was still standing, and the competitors had turned to dust.

How can you learn from a case study like that?

Learn from the mistakes, not the success. Learn from how people fail. A lot of MBA schools teach successful case studies. When you read too many successful case studies, do you think you can be successful? No! There are a lot of things that you don't know.[10]

Entrepreneurship, Jack argues, is not about how many successes you experience, but how many failures and mistakes you overcome. The key to unlocking the Alibaba Unicorn lies in understanding the social influence that comes from Jack's repeated willingness to fail and ability to convince others to fail with him.

I still remember the first time I met Jack Ma. It was 2017 and I had been selected as one of four US delegates to attend the World Internet Conference at the Wuzhen Institute in China. For three days I attended coffee conversations and keynote addresses from leaders in the technology world: Chris O'Neill (the former CEO of Evernote, a $2 billion company); Sundar Pichai (the current CEO of Google); and every CEO of "BATH companies" (a collection of China's most valuable technology companies, Baidu, Alibaba, Tencent, and Huawei).

Each shared their perspectives on the future of the technology world. These other executives were practical, rooted in data and facts. Jack was not. Compared to the other executives, he was a philosophical loose cannon. He said what he thought with no remorse, a risky thing to do in an authoritarian state like China. While most of what he said was not politically correct or acceptable, it was emotional: focused on *how* to live rather than *what* to do. His stories contained lessons learned from failure that were as timeless as African proverbs and as memorable as the lines of Confucius. How he had thrived as a business executive in China was a mystery to me and apparently to the thousands of other conference attendees who wanted to hear from him.

Jack hosted his talk in secret: invite-only and at 7:00 a.m. on the last day of the conference, which traditionally started at 10:00 a.m. The three other American college delegates and I heard through the grapevine about the talk and woke up at 5:00 a.m. to sneak in and secure a spot in the fifty-person room. We found a set of chairs in the middle, crumpled up the "reserved seat" signs, and settled in to hear what wisdom this mogul would have to share.

The room murmured as groggy journalists, Chinese government officials, and executives filed into the room to their assigned seats. Unfortunately, four of them weren't allowed in since we took their seats: whoops! Then, like a spark, the buzz silenced. He needed no introduction. It was Jack Ma.

I, however, was shocked: this man was supposedly one of the wealthiest, most powerful, most innovative men in China? He looked about 5 foot 3 inches (I suppose one inch for every billion dollars that he's worth) with a head that looked more suited for a Lego figure than an adult-sized body. He bounded up the steps with a beaming smile and radiated energy despite the bags under his eyes. His suit was crisp: not flashy, but clean enough to signal that it wasn't grabbed off a clothing hanger two years ago at Macy's like mine. He grabbed the mic and began speaking.

Don't be scared of failure. My asset is my failure stories. There are a lot of stories about us, about me. But none of the books I read about me talk about my failures. Someday I may write a book whose name is 'Alibaba: 1,001 Mistakes.' This is the best asset that you have: to learn from your mistakes, to learn from others' mistakes, not because you want to avoid the mistakes but because when you face these mistakes you will know how to face it and how to challenge it. This is critical.[11]

THE SCIENCE OF FAILURE

For entrepreneurs, failure is an expectation. On average eleven out of every twelve startups fail, a 2019 startup ecosystem report describes. It's easier to get into Harvard Business School than it is to make a successful startup. And yet, every year over 472 million entrepreneurs worldwide attempt to run 305 million companies, with about 100 million new businesses starting each year.[12] Even if you're risk averse and don't want to fail, failure is a required fact of life in creating a startup company, and especially if you want to create a billion-dollar company.

"But what if I have money from a venture capitalist?" you exclaim. "Surely, my chance of failure would be lower!" That's only marginally true. Surprisingly, 75 percent of venture-backed companies never return cash to their investors and 30-40 percent lose all their investors' initial investments. In a portfolio of one hundred companies, venture capitalists can expect nine successful startups, one potential unicorn, and ninety failures.[13]

"So then," the startup folklore goes, "the more you fail the better!" Well...Sort of.

According to Paul Gompers of the Harvard Business School, just as success begets more success, failure begets more failure. His research published in April 2010 found that previously failed entrepreneurs were no more likely to succeed than first-time entrepreneurs. These same results were confirmed by a study of German entrepreneurs by researchers at the investment bank KfW Bankengruppe who found that entrepreneurs who started a company after a failure performed *more poorly* compared with other founders.

Knowing this, how is Jack still so adamant that failure allowed him to succeed? How did he defy statistics and studies?

THE FORCED DEVELOPMENT OF GUANXI

Jack's failures began early. In fact, his first failure was the situational luck of what family he was born into.

His father and mother were both poor and worked as musicians. Together, their pay was no more than $6 a month or, in a good month, $8. This sum was stretched to feed the mouths of six people: Jack, his father, his mother, his grandfather, his brother, and his sister. No one expected Jack to amount to anything. He should, realistically, have become a menial worker like his parents and made no more than $6,000 over the course of his life.

With my background, my family background, with my education background. I would be like a -2 or -3 on a scale of -10 to +10. Honestly, because I know who I am, from my father, my mother and my ancestors, nobody in my family is a government officer or a business leader. That is why the past twenty years, we never got even $0.01 from (the) government or $0.01 from the (Chinese) banks. In theory, no matter how hard I worked, I probably would only have gotten a +2 or a +3: that's my top. But today, I'm a +6 or more, so the +4 difference, that does not belong to me. That's not me.[14]

Perhaps not, I thought as I leaned in deeper to hear the rest of Jack's story.

Despite his background, Jack was immensely curious about the world around him at a time when China was also becoming more curious about the world. Growing up in Hangzhou in 1978, Jack was exposed to the foreigners who flooded the banks of the West Lake after Deng Xiaoping's and Richard Nixon's diplomatic relationship to connect China with the world. Every morning for the next nine years, Jack rode his bicycle to the Hangzhou Hotel where he befriended foreign visitors and practiced English with them.[15]

Even though Jack had street smarts, he was quick to realize that he was not book smart and actually was quite bad at school. Instead, Jack focused on developing Guanxi, a Chinese word for the system of social networks and influential relationships that help to facilitate business and power. Guanxi for Jack was a lifestyle: since he knew he would never be the richest or smartest in the room, he pivoted to winning respect through helping others. Empowering others as a means to empower himself.

I know people. I know what people want. I know what people don't want. When I was a student in the university, I was not a good student. That's why I really don't like a lot of good students.[16]

He winked at the crowd who laughed at his joke on cue.

Growing up, Jack was always tenth or fifteenth in class and between primary school and university he failed three times.

When he finally arrived in the university, he resolved that he would not "spend time trying to be the number one but try to be the number one person that can help and work with people".[17]

Jack was elected as the chairman of the Students' Union and later became the chairman of the Students' Union for the whole city, where he oversaw 100,000 students. His job was to work with the people and to listen to people from a position of no influence. "The only thing you want to win," he reflected, "is respect by supporting other people."

By all means, despite the titles, Jack failed at school: he wasn't a good student. His success was in mastering how to empower others to be better students: Guanxi.

Eventually Jack graduated from the university, not as the best student or as the worst student, and his failure continued. He applied to over thirty jobs and was rejected from almost all of them: He applied to KFC with twenty-four classmates, twenty-three got the job and he was the only reject. He applied to the police force with five classmates, again four got jobs, and he was the only reject. As a nail in the coffin, after waiting in a two-hour queue with his cousin to be a waiter at a four-star hotel in Hangzhou, he was rejected while his cousin, who had lower scores, was accepted for the position. These moments of rejection, while painful, were preparing Jack for a career in business akin to boxing: one where the only way to win is to get hit.

Finally, after almost three dozen rejections, Jack landed his first job as an English teacher (an homage to his early days learning English from tourists). His secret to being a good teacher in his three years of teaching was to finish class five minutes early.

No matter how wonderful you teach, if you spend five extra minutes teaching then students don't like you.[18]

His hack allowed him to be elected as the best teacher at his university for three years in a row; another bout of Guanxi.

One thing I learned from teachers, and later when I become a CEO, is that a good teacher always expects his students to be better than him. The teacher wants his students to be a banker, a mayor, or a scientist; you don't want your students to be bankrupt or in jail. You always expect your students to be better. This is what I learned when I became an entrepreneur. I always want to hire the good people who are smarter than I am and always make sure that they are better than I am.[19]

Where Gompers and other researchers are correct is in recognizing that failure for its own sake does not increase a founder's ability to be successful. However, what they miss in studying failure is that the social relationships and social acumen that entrepreneurs often build from failing is more important than the failure itself. For Jack, his failures allowed him to realize that skill and talent alone would not bring him success; instead, he needed to empower others. His failure developed Guanxi.

Ronald S. Burt and Katarzyna Burzynska, joint researchers from Chicago and Sweden, correlate these findings in their 2017 study of 700 entrepreneurs in Shanghai, China. They found that "higher trust and being strategically connected (having *Guanxi*, or broker networks) was correlated to business success with those Chinese entrepreneurs".[20]

Guanxi exists everywhere. In the private sector of the United States and Western Europe, estimates suggest that 80 percent of jobs are found through personal networks.[21] Even in the public sector, Washington, DC can best be described as a revolving door of politicians turned lobbyists and consultants with ties to regulatory agencies who have the influence to shape government policy.[22] It's no surprise: all over the world, your network is your net worth.

For Jack Ma, in spite of academic and situational failures, his repeated success developed from his desire to build strong networks.

JACK'S GUANXI GOING GLOBAL

During his time as a teacher, Jack was presented with an opportunity to serve as a translator for a project in the United States. When he arrived in Los Angeles, Jack discovered that the US partner he was sent to work with was a con man. Knowing no one in California, Jack fled to Seattle to stay with a family he knew (did someone say Guanxi?). As he was there, he had an encounter that would change his life.

My friend Stuart said to me, "Jack. There's this internet. You can find whatever you want through the internet."

I said "Really?" and searched the word 'Beer.'

A very simple word, 'Beer.' I do not know why I searched 'Beer,' but I found American beer, German beer, and no Chinese beers. I was curious. So, I searched 'China.' The search engine said, 'No China.' I was shocked. 'No China?'

I told my friend, "We (can) make a Chinese homepage and post that inside the search engine to see the translated results." So, I made the 'Hope Translation Agency' home page, a very ugly looking homepage. At 9:30 p.m. we launched it. By 12:00 a.m. I received five emails: three from the USA, one from Japan, and one from Germany. I was so excited. I said, "This is something interesting!" [23]

It was the first time he had seen a computer, but this encounter sparked a new drive in Jack. Just as he was getting used to success as a teacher for twelve dollars a month (more than both of his parents' salaries), he decided to risk it all in 1994 by quitting his job to start "ChinaPages."

Spoiler alert: just like in the rest of his life, Jack failed.

When Jack started ChinaPages, he would go knocking on the doors of government officials hoping to drum up support for the internet and for his business. It was the first internet business to ever be launched in China. Dubious that the internet even existed, government officials and investors turned him away saying that what he was doing wasn't appropriate or realistic. "You should maybe just go back to teaching English".[24]

I went back to China with the Seattle dream of (the) internet. I believed this thing is going to change the world. I believed this thing will be big, but whether 'Jack Ma and his team can be successful,' I didn't know. I told the team somebody will be successful, but not us. It may not be us. So, tough days in China in the years 1996, 1997, and then we went nowhere.[25]

Jack borrowed $2,000 from friends, family, and relatives to bring the dream to life. Unfortunately, they competed with China Telecom who had more money and social connections. Being a startup, Jack and his team were "unkillable" but couldn't win the battle against them either.

So we had a joint venture, they have 70 percent we have 30 percent. And I was so stupid: I thought "They really love us," but they got us because they wanted to kill us. Of our seven board seats, they got five. Without even seeing our ideas they would say "We don't like it." So I…thought to myself "Maybe I should go into Beijing and join the government, maybe they can help us in promoting the internet".[26]

It was 1997 and Jack gave up on being a startup founder. Instead, he pivoted to work as a government employee to change his country (and unbeknownst to him, the world) from within. Again, another failure.

He went to Beijing and joined the Ministry of Foreign Trade as part of a fourteen-month job contract.

There, I realized that the working side of a government can never, ever, ever promote or make the internet business because the philosophy of the internet is to help <u>other</u> people develop their own businesses. But the government, they wanted control at that time. So, it was two totally different philosophies.

The government is smart, they are good people, but they often think "How can I use the internet to manage and control?" But we thought that the internet should not be about control but should be used to help people develop. And then I thought, "Well, no chance in the government, but I don't believe we should give up." So I was desperate and I was thinking a lot.[27]

Jack went back to Hangzhou conflicted: Was a startup even worth it? If he'd failed once with the government, why even try again? Would it be useful to risk another failure?

GUANXI SEEDING ALIBABA

On February 21, 1999, Jack made his decision by inviting eighteen of his friends, colleagues, and students to be his co-founders for a new project.[28] They took a video of the moment: the start of Alibaba. In the grainy video reminiscent of the dot-com bubble, a thirty-five-year-old Jack Ma predicts that in twenty years, this site would be one of the top ten sites of the world and that Alibaba would be a company built in China but designed for the world.

As Jack described to the intimate conference audience with a chuckle, "I was a blind man riding on the back of blind tigers".[29]

The story of Alibaba after this point is long and filled with even more failures, mistakes, and adventures: Guerrilla Warfare with eBay in the early 2000s, a $1 billion cash-injection from Yahoo, and a secretive project named 'TaoBao' that saved the company. But these sorts of lessons of how innovators like Jack *built* their companies will be discussed in depth later in this book as we understand the *refinement* and *execution* process of Unlocking Unicorns. For now, the goal is to deeply understand the *exploration* behind Alibaba. How did Jack *see and anticipate* this startup idea when no one else did?

Jack received his inspiration for Alibaba by his failure and social connections: he failed as a student and became a teacher, he failed in his ChinaPages startup then pivoted to government, and even today he sees his company as one that thrives only because it actively tries to foresee failures before they appear and develop the social connections necessary to create success. Rather than taking the spotlight as a success, Jack has thrived in being the non-sexy guy who empowers small businesses to achieve their goals and dreams in life. For Jack, inspiration comes through Guanxi, enabling ordinary people through social influence (and an appetite for failure) to achieve incredible feats that they never thought possible.

I'm a very lucky person. In my apartment I talked to eighteen young people like me. We wanted to build up a company using the internet to help make doing business easier, using the internet to support every small business. To support every young person and every woman so that if they have a dream, if they have some ideas, we will enable them to make their dream come true to sell their products all over the world. That was in the year 1999, in my apartment. Well very few people believed that, but we made it happen. I'm a very, very lucky person.[30]

The key to Unlocking the Alibaba Unicorn is in Jack Ma's failure-inspired Guanxi.

Chapter Summary

Lesson 1. Eleven out of every twelve startups fail. This is true even if a founder has made a company in the past: in fact, studies from Paul Gompers and KfW Bankengruppe have confirmed that past startup failure tends to beget more startup failure. Even with money from venture-backed companies, the odds for creating a successful startup are slim: 75 percent of venture-backed companies never return cash to their investors.

Lesson 2. Contrary to these studies, Jack Ma's career has been enabled by failure. Rather than failing aimlessly, Jack embraced strategic failure. This phenomenon is supported by Ronald S. Burt and Katarzyna Burzynska of Chicago and Sweden who find that higher trust and connection is correlated to business success. Jack used each failed opportunity as a way to develop his Guanxi (or business network). Startup founders should take a similar approach by actively "failing forward" with intentional learnings, useful connections, and transferable skills from every experience.

Lesson 3. The idea behind Alibaba was actually inspired by a trip to America where Jack realized that there were no Chinese beers being shipped to America. While the initial idea failed, it planted the seed for further success. One way to discover billion-dollar startup ideas is by plugging gaps that exist between emerging markets and developed markets.

CHAPTER 2:

CONTRARIAN CHALLENGER

———

Scrolling through LinkedIn, I stumbled upon an interesting quote from Jarrid Tingle, the founder of Harlem Capital, a venture capital firm with more than $175 million in assets under management. He wrote that "If you do average things, expect average results".[31] For him, success came not from following the crowd but in taking the risk to go up to bat, even with the chance of striking out.

As I leaned back in my creaky, black desk chair I mulled over Jarrid's claim in my mind. It clashed with another adage from legendary investor and oracle of Omaha, Warren Buffet who argues that "It is not necessary to do *extraordinary* things to get *extraordinary* results." Consistency and the accumulation of small wins over time, Warren argues, is the crux of success. It's a snowball effect, not a home run.

So, which of these two philosophies is the one to adopt when trying to maximize your ability to create a Unicorn? Perhaps the best way to gauge this is by looking at an individual who has received extraordinary results throughout her life through using both of these tactics. Today, she is the *only* self-made female billionaire in India, was India's first female brewmaster, and was the first Indian woman to join Warren Buffet and Bill Gates' "giving pledge" to donate a majority of her wealth to charity before she dies.[32] She founded the largest biotech company in Asia and has been featured as *Time's* 100 Most Influential People, *Forbes'* 100 Most Powerful Women, *Financial Times'* Top 50 Women in Business, and the 2020 EY Entrepreneur of the Year.[33]

Her name is Kiran Mazumdar-Shaw.

She is a Unicorn founder and is the perfect example for understanding how to turn average expectations into extraordinary results. Today, her business, Biocon, is a multi-million-dollar empire that makes drugs for cancer, diabetes, and other life-threatening illnesses. Quite an accomplishment for a business that started in a garage with $200.

The key to understanding Kiran's success lies in understanding her contrarianism. She was raised to be a contrarian person, sought to surround herself with co-contrarians, and took contrarian actions to amass a personal wealth of more than $4.7 billion. For her, the secret lies not in doing "average things" or "extraordinary things" for their own sake, but in consistently challenging the things that make the status quo.

She brings a whole new meaning to the old adage, "If I only had a penny for every time someone doubted me...."

BEING CONTRARIAN

Kiran was not born a contrarian, but quickly became one through her father's influence. Born in 1953, she grew up as the daughter of a Brewmaster father and homemaker mother in Bangalore, South India, also known as the Garden City of India. As she reflects,

It was a great place to grow up because it was cosmopolitan (and) a very modern city in India. It was also the science capital of India. In Bangalore we had the famous Indian Institute of Science and the National Aeronautical Laboratory and there was a Science Museum, which we used to frequent quite a lot. As kids, we grew up loving science. I'm really glad I grew up in Bangalore.[34]

Kiran, her parents, and her two brothers lived in the United Breweries staff compound surrounded by the mash of malted barley, the heat of aromatic hops, and the bubbling of fermented yeast. In between hide-and-seek games around tins and kettles with her brothers, Kiran attended private school at Bishop Cotton Girls' School and later attended college at Mount Carmel College, Bangalore.[35] While both of these schools were designed for young girls and women, Kiran was constantly reminded by her father that "You must look at life the same way your brothers do. Don't think that you have to look at it differently just because you're my daughter or just because you're a girl".[36]

Kiran's father raised his children as though he had three sons despite the heavily sexist society that saturated India at the time and continues to affect life today. These constant reminders were the guardrails that kept Kiran on a path to constantly challenge the status quo.

She double majored in biology and zoology, and despite having dreams of attending medical school, failed to pass her scholarship test. With no contingency plan in place, Kiran's father (then a managing director at United Breweries) suggested that she follow in his footsteps to become a brewmaster.

At the time, there were no female brewmasters in India. While Kiran saw it as a profession that was odd and disconcerting for a girl, her father argued that "brewing is the oldest biotechnology known to man".[37] "It's not a gender issue," he reasoned, "if you like science you should do brewing because it's a science...a fermentation science...a life science".[38] Hesitant, but excited and pushed by her father's guidance, Kiran packed her bags and left home to attend Ballarat University in Australia to learn the family craft. When she arrived, she was the only woman in a class of all men.

That was quite a defining time in my life, I would say. I learned to fend for myself not only as a young woman in an all-male class, but also as someone who was pursuing a very, very different vocation which no woman would think of pursuing. I certainly got my spunk from my Australian days: I learned to drink with the boys, I learned to do well at class, and I used to talk about my projects all the time so that gave me a terrific sense of success and achievement and confidence. I would say more than anything else, I came back (to Bangalore) very, very self-assured.[39]

Kiran's situation of flying in the face of gender norms is expected for any Indian woman looking to enter the workforce. According to the World Bank, only 65 percent of women are literate as compared to 80 percent of men. Moreover, even though women made up 48 percent of the Indian population in 2019, India has one of the lowest female labor force participation rates in the world with less than a third of women–fifteen years or older–working or actively looking for a job.[40] It ranks 120th among 131 countries. For Indian women looking to be an entrepreneur, the numbers aren't much better. Only about 14 percent of Indian women own or run businesses, according to the Sixth Economic Census, conducted in 2014 (as compared to 43 percent in the United States).[41]

Even today, these statistics are bleak. So how did Kiran break the mold in the male-dominated brewing industry of the 1970s?

One of the key takeaways is that Kiran was not a conformist. In psychology, conformity is defined as the tendency to change one's beliefs or behaviors in ways consistent with the group norm or standard.[42] Since humans are inherently social animals, we tend to yield to perceived group pressure even if no direct request or command is made (unlike compliance where others request that one do something or obedience where one follows orders).

In fact, Kiran is what most psychologists would call "anti-conformist." As most famously discovered by Solomon Asch in his 1951 line judgement experiments, there tend to be three types of reactions from participants in evolving situations of conformity. Two are expected: those who remain independent despite feeling uncomfortable and those that conform. However, a third (and small group) was surprising: those who were anti-conformists and slavish contrarians. Rather than conforming or non-conforming, they did precisely the opposite of what the group did. They conformed to anti-conformity.

Kiran, and successful anomalous unicorn founders in general, must strive to be *anti-conformist* in the face of societal norms. Especially when an individual is the first or only in the room, they must be anti-conformist for its own sake. As Kiran exhibited, they must not just practice contrarianism out of convenience, instead they must be anti-conformist as a habit and way of being.

Perhaps Kiran saw herself a bit like her father, who himself had gone against the grain by becoming a brewmaster despite being the only son of a very Orthodox Gujarati Brahmin family where even the word alcohol was taboo. Upon return to India, even her father's mother (Kiran's grandmother) remarked, "Your father does not have two sons and a daughter, he has three sons." With her parents' support and her extended family's blessing, Kiran was ready to take on the world.[43] However, the world was not ready for her.

TEAM OF CONTRARIANS

Though Kiran returned to India as the top graduate from her brewing class, she struggled to get a full-time job. "I knocked at almost every brewery I could to give me a job," Kiran recalls.[44] She saw some traction for a few years getting short contracts from breweries who wanted her to solve short-term problems for them, but none would hire her for a permanent role. All her rejectors gave her three responses, and each focused on her gender. First, she consistently heard that as a woman it would be tough to have Kiran as part of an all-male management. Second, these breweries worried that it would be tough to have Kiran participate in unions that, while strong, did not feel comfortable dealing with a woman. And third, breweries worried that many employees did not want to work for a young, twenty-five-year-old woman as their manager.

Oh, and every brewery said this to her face.[45]

The rude shock was the awakening that it wasn't going to be possible for Kiran to become a brewmaster in India. "I was trying to do something rebellious at that time. I was trying to do something to change society's attitude to women".[46] But there came a point when she had to throw in the towel: "That failure helped me to realize that I've got to do something else".[47] Kiran planned to leave India to pursue her brewing career in a more gender-friendly environment like Scotland to carry on the family business.

However, just as she was about to pack up and leave, Kiran had a chance encounter that changed her life.

Leslie Auchincloss, the founder of Irish enzyme maker Biocon Biochemicals, was looking for a partner in India and had heard of the only Indian woman in a class of men who graduated number one from an Australian university. He sought her out and gave Kiran the pitch:

They (Leslie Auchincloss and Biocon Biochemicals) were actually buying an enzyme extracted from papaya. A lot of this crude papain was coming from India. Therefore, they felt that if they could start up a company in India that could refine that papain and make the final product, it (would make) more sense (and money). He was someone who had heard about me because of my Australian days, and he tracked me down and said, "Why don't you partner with me?".[48]

Auchincloss' idea was to create industrial enzymes for makers of beer, food, and textiles around the world by growing microbes in large vats under precise temperatures and pressures. Kiran, hesitant, did not accept immediately.

My first response was "I don't think I'm the right partner because (A) I'm a woman (B) I don't have money and (C) I don't have business experience, so I think you're making a big mistake." But he basically was looking for someone who had fire in the belly who could be very passionate about starting a business and running a business. He wanted a young entrepreneur.[49]

After weighing her options, Kiran convinced herself that the biotechnology Auchincloss wanted her to implement was actually quite similar to brewing since they both were "actually a very enzymatic process".[50] She mulled it over and decided to team up with a fellow contrarian to build something bigger than both of them. Of course, it was risky for Auchincloss as well, but his bet on Kiran was a bet on her contrarian character rather than the culture of the day.

It was the beginning of Kiran, the "accidental" entrepreneur.

For any women in business reading this book, these stories about Kiran are not surprising. Even though there are 114 percent more female entrepreneurs today globally than there were twenty years ago, women are still becoming entrepreneurs out of necessity rather than from opportunity.[51] A 2019 Global Entrepreneurship Monitor report coauthored by researchers from Babson College and Smith College found that while 74 percent of men start companies to "pursue an opportunity" only 68 percent of women do the same thing.[52]

This "6 percent gender gap" is caused by a myriad of factors, but focus on societal norms. Women in the corporate settings globally are paid less, have less control over their schedules, and face discrimination in ways that men don't have to. Thus, like Kiran, many turn to entrepreneurship as a way to thrive outside of the established, and often sexist, business ecosystem.

However, even as entrepreneurs, women still face challenges. According to a 2020 study by Crunchbase, only 2 percent of all venture capital funding was provided to female-only founded companies in 2020—a 5 percent decline from 2018.[53] Having a male co-founder doesn't help much either: companies co-founded with a male and female team received a slightly-higher 9 percent of venture funding in 2020—essentially staying flat over the last decade. Systematically, women are at a disadvantage when fundraising.

In such a system, being a contrarian and partnering with co-contrarian team members who have access can increase opportunities for success. More importantly, however, Kiran's story and these statistics show the importance of allies in creating outsized impact as an underrepresented female founder. As a member of a systemically advantaged group (whether caused by race, gender, or another factor), advantaged allies have an opportunity to empower those who would normally be overlooked.

While Kiran is the lead on stage, Leslie Auchincloss also played a significant role in setting the scene of Biocon by supporting a contrarian challenger.

RECRUITING CO-CONTRARIANS

Excited and undaunted, Kiran secured the required permits and set up shop in her garage. Biocon India was incorporated in 1978 and despite not being able to get any investment from banks (they all felt lending to a young woman in the unknown "biotech industry" was risky), she launched the business with an initial investment of 10,000 Indian rupees ($200). The only thing left to do was get employees.[54]

Knowing the culture of the day, Kiran threw in a few half-white lies to get applications flowing in the door. Her advertisements read "Managing Director of a Multinational Company is Looking for Secretarial Help" or "Multinational Company Looking for an Accountant;" however, as soon as employees would arrive at the garage, they would be extremely disappointed.[55] For almost five dozen interviews every exchange was the same.

They would take one look at Kiran, and assuming she was the secretary, say "Well, we have an appointment with the managing director."

"Yes, that's me," Kiran would respond.

After seeing their look of shock as they stood in her garage, Kiran would follow this up by saying, "What can I do for you? Let's get the interview started".[56]

Within minutes, every interview turned in the same way. Rather than Kiran interviewing the candidate, it was the candidate interviewing her about job security, working for a woman, and the future of a company headed by a woman. Surprisingly, even women who Kiran interviewed had the same concerns. "I realized that, even then, I couldn't get people to join me," Kiran reflects with an exasperated sigh.[57]

Her frown then turns to a slight smirk, "The first couple of years were very challenging, but it was fun. I took it on in a very amusing way as a child would do, saying 'Let me prove these ignorant minds wrong. Let me educate them about what it's all about,'".[58]

Finally, she hired three employees: a pair of semi-retired mechanics who worked at a tractor company but were willing to join Kiran because she paid them more, and an old friend who agreed to take sabbatical from their teaching job to double up as her secretary.[59] This traction reassured a few skeptical bankers who felt more comfortable lending her money as well.

Today, it's laughable to think that people were hesitant to work for or with Kiran. Her business employs over 7,500 of the smartest people in India with 10 percent PhDs, 45 percent master's, and 33 percent bachelor's degree holders amongst her employees. Her company contains the brains of India.[60]

In creating these jobs, Kiran did not settle for those who were willing to just go with the flow. She desired to find, and successfully found a team of contrarians who were willing to challenge the status quo with her. They believed in her vision , and more importantly, they believed in her. If not for surrounding herself with other supportive co-contrarians, Biocon probably would not have grown to the scale it is today.

"I could have been a job seeker, but now I am a job creator".[61]

Globally, over 252 million women around the world are entrepreneurs and 153 million women are operating established businesses.[62] Like Kiran, they are job creators. In the US alone where 11.6 million women owned businesses, female entrepreneurs employ nearly 9 million people to generate over $1.7 trillion in revenue.[63] Every day, each and every one of these founders and employees is challenging the status quo.

ACTING CONTRARIAN

The first year of the business was a huge success. The microbial enzymes that Kiran was producing for Leslie proved successful, and she developed aspirations to develop a whole new branch of the business focused on plant enzymes. In a move that many of her peers saw as irrational, Kiran decided to purchase a twenty-acre plot of land with all the savings her business had earned in its first year.

Everyone looked at me saying, "What on earth are you doing buying such a big piece of land? You will hardly be able to use half an acre!" I said, "Yeah, that's true. But let me figure it out: it's going so cheap that I should buy it. Let's hope that one day I'll use up all those twenty!".[64]

That contrarian vision which Kiran acted upon ultimately paid off. By 1983, just five years after the business was started and one year after purchasing the land, this Gujarati businesswoman had moved her offices to that plot of land.[65] Today, they use every bit of that property and have purchased one hundred more acres in India and fifty acres in Malaysia to double-down on their plant-based enzyme business.

Even though she never went to business school, Kiran retained a keen business sense, and when given the chance in 1989 to buy out her partners, became the sole owner of the business. With no one else to report to, she expanded the business again by creating biosimilars (the biotech equivalent of generic drugs) in addition to plant and microbial enzymes.[66] Under Kiran's eye, they doubled down on investing heavily in research and development in the early 1990s to spend 10 percent annually on patents and new drug types.[67]

Rather than following the traditional model of drug companies, which is to recoup R&D costs by selling drugs in countries willing to pay higher prices, Kiran has turned that model on its head opting instead to sell drugs that cost less to many more people in less developed countries.[68]

A successful drug is not a $1 billion drug; it's a drug that helps 1 billion people.[69]

Kiran has pioneered the biotech sector in India. In 2004, this was cemented in history: Kiran took her company public and by the end of the first day of trading, her company was valued at more than $1 billion; only the second Indian company *ever* to break that ceiling.[70]

It was a sort of Eureka moment. I'd never realized that we had created this kind of value.... It was a great feeling, and it was great that we had created this kind of value with all these efforts we had put in over the last, you know, twenty-five years. It was a wonderful time and an inflection point for me because it was about value creation. It was about wealth creation. It was about making sure that a whole bunch of us who had worked so hard to build the company to where it was got rewarded.... There was a sense of pride that India's first biotech company had come of age.[71]

THE CONTRARIAN CHALLENGER

As successful as she is today, Kiran's path was never predetermined. But it was certainly paved by the intentional decisions to be a contrarian every step along the way despite societal pressures to conform.

As an entrepreneur, I have always believed in differentiation.
I've always felt that you've got to be differentiated and different
to stand apart. But if you want to do that there is intrinsic risk
because you're trying to do something that has never been tried
before. The fact that I pioneered the biotech sector in India
shows you that I was willing to experiment and take this big
wild risk which nobody had attempted before. But I think the
risk is also about understanding what you're getting into.[72]

Even if she didn't know all the twists and turns that her journey would take her on, Kiran's support from her mother (who
also became an entrepreneur at the age of sixty-eight) and
father (who supported her as though she were a son) was a
key to kindling the contrarian flame within Kiran.[73] Eventually, this flame led Kiran to both surround herself with
contrarian influences and hire co-contrarians to ultimately
act in a contrarian way to achieve outsized returns.

To Kiran, both Jarrid Tingle and Warren Buffet are right.
Extraordinary results come from challenging the status quo.
They come from being contrarian. At times, this means not
doing the average task but at other times it means consistently working to push your beliefs forward. What matters
most, and the key to unlocking the Biocon Unicorn, is to
become a contrarian thinker, surround yourself with contrarian influences, and smartly take contrarian actions.

Entrepreneurship isn't a snowball or a baseball, it's a mara-
thon: "Failure is temporary, but giving up is final".[74]

Chapter Summary

Lesson 1. For entrepreneurs building startups in an environment where the odds are against them, contrarianism is an invaluable personality trait to embrace. Kiran Mazumdar-Shaw was a daughter born in a culture of sons; however, from a young age she was groomed to be a contrarian by her father who treated her as if she were a son. In her career she went against the grain by joining the 14 percent of Indian women who own or run their own business. She was what most psychologists would describe as "anti-conformist."

Lesson 2. Unlike male entrepreneurs, female entrepreneurs tend to create companies out of necessity rather than from opportunity. In their 2019 global entrepreneurship monitor report, Babson College and Smith College called this gender gap in why entrepreneurs make their companies "the 6 percent gap." The gap only widens when examining startup funding in the space. Female-only startup founders received 2 percent of all venture capital funding in 2020 and are often systematically disadvantaged. The disparities of gender-based entrepreneurship can't be solved by any individual, but an anti-conformist mentality can push female founders to success despite the odds.

Lesson 3. The ability to be a generalist and cross-apply skills can lead to unique business insights and advantages that allow startup founders to out-innovate, out-perform, and outpace competition. Kiran, for instance, cross-applied brewing to biotechnology and has sought to be a job creator rather than a job seeker due to her parents' influence.

CHAPTER 3:

SANGUINE SEER

I sometimes play a game where I try to predict the future. "Assuming I had unlimited money," I ask myself, "which country would I 'buy' to experience the greatest return in fifty years?"

Take a minute and run through the thought experiment. What metrics matter to you? Which investment philosophies do you find yourself gravitating toward?

For me, the three parameters I fall back on are growth, capital, and innovation. More often than not, I adopt the perspective of Benjamin Graham, who preached about value investing. His philosophy argues that investors should buy assets that are currently undervalued by the market and hold until the rest of the world sees it. This philosophy led Warren Buffet to double- and triple-down on companies like Coca-Cola, GEICO, and See's Candy with impressive results. In my thought experiment, fifty years, I think, should be more than enough time for my choice of country to produce returns like Buffet or Graham.

So, what country would I buy that's undervalued on growth, capital, and innovation today?

First, I'd narrow in on a continent: specifically, the African continent. In 2019, investment in African-based startups topped $1 billion for the first time ever with more than ninety African-based companies raising more than $1 million in funding.[75] With over 500 million African citizens logging on to the internet every month, the fastest-growing middle class in the world, and a trend of Pan-African initiatives, some estimate that the African continent could contribute $3 trillion of total GDP through continental free trade agreements.[76] Broadened in context, this would make Africa the largest free trade region in the world.[77]

Zeroing in on Africa, one country excites me especially. Despite being a proud Ghanaian, I put my chips all-in on Nigeria (Sorry, Mom. It's still West Africa, so maybe that counts?)

Hear me out.

In mid-2017, about 1.25 billion people lived in Africa, and Nigeria was the most populous nation on the continent with 202 million people.[78] By 2050, experts estimate that Nigeria will be the third most populous nation in the world.[79] Primarily, it's fueled by fertility: between 2008 and 2018, the fertility rate in Nigeria was more than 5.5 children per possible mother.[80] The United States' is 1.7, for comparison.[81]

Nigeria is also the largest economy in Africa. In 2019, its Gross Domestic Product (GDP) was $410 billion.[82] $100 billion more than South Africa and nearly twice that of Egypt.

But, in my hypothetical game, population and spending alone are not reasons to make an investment. One of the biggest key factors is entrepreneurial spirit.

On this metric, Nigeria wins. By a long shot.

The 2020 Economist Pocketbook of Figures reported that Nigeria had the highest percentage of owner-managers of any country in the world. "39.9% of the population is an entrepreneur: either full-time or by-the-side,".[83]

This thought experiment often makes me realize when I'm late to the party. However, Mitchell Elegbe has seen things clearly for years. He founded Interswitch, a payment processing company, in 2002 with headquarters in Lagos, Nigeria. Seventeen years later, on November 11, 2019, Interswitch received an investment from Visa and became one of the less than ten Unicorn companies in Africa.[84] The company was valued at over $1 billion: about one dollar for every African citizen.

When you look at Africa and Nigeria what do you see? Mitchell Elegbe, the sanguine seer, is clear:

We don't see a dark continent. We see a continent that has the opportunity to use Science and Technology to invest in renewable energy and provide electricity with clean energy better than every other place in the world. Coming from behind does not make you bad. It allows you to learn from the mistakes of others and improve your environment. I see opportunities for better housing. I see opportunities for better schools. I see opportunities for modern health care facilities. What do you see? What is your perspective?.[85]

Mitchell's enthusiasm implies that Unicorns in Africa won't be rare in the future. Perhaps we shouldn't even think of them as Unicorns but instead as zebras with a horn: a much more common phenomenon. If one just adjusts their perspective, opportunity is everywhere, and it is common. Mitchell has mastered what he calls the "three different kinds of sight: hindsight, insight, and foresight,".[86] Unzipping the horned Interswitch zebra is a case study in understanding these three types of optimism that allowed Mitchell to thrive in building a unicorn company.

HINDSIGHT

You need hindsight to understand things that have happened in the past. Your past experiences will shape the kind of insights you get. That insight will influence the kind of foresight you have.[87]

Growing up as the last child in his family, Mitchell was both unlucky and lucky. Unluckily, his father passed away while his mother was pregnant with him. Luckily, Mitchell and his siblings were raised by their uncles.[88] Dr. Burian Carew, Mitchell's uncle, was the co-founder of Nigeria's Telnet group, and played the role of father in his life. "If you are looking at rich from the terms of material wealth, I won't say I come from a rich home but if you are looking at rich in terms of values, yes!" he exclaimed.[89]

He did well in school and went on to pursue an undergraduate degree in Electrical Engineering from the University of Benin. As a student with no father at home, Mitchell had to find a way to pay for school himself. He decided to make ends meet by creating a business out of dubbing cassettes he borrowed from friends.[90] Every week, he would commute for over two hours from Benin City to Onitsha to buy high quality audio tapes, record on them in a recording studio, and sell these tapes in school.[91] It was a good money-making scheme for a time, but eventually the business ran into problems.

Not too long afterwards, other students began doing the same thing, recording on tapes of lower quality, which totally wiped out my profits. Then I switched over to selling shirts. This is how I learnt how to read a market, and also time management, lessons that have become invaluable to me today.[92]

Despite this entrepreneurial mind, Mitchell did not dive into starting a company immediately. After graduating and a year of volunteering through the mandatory National Youth Service Corps (NYSC), Mitchell moved to Scotland to work at Schlumberger Wireline & Testing as a Field Engineer.

(Going to) Scotland was my first time leaving the country. I had never flown out of the country before. That was the first visa I had ever got. I thought "This was my dream playing out in front of me." If you went to the University of Benin and did engineering, you'd be a very miserable person if you did not work in the oil and gas industry. I wanted to work for Shell, Chevron, Mobil, or Schlumberger. That was the dream then, so I had to follow that passion too![93]

Unfortunately, despite achieving his dream, when Mitchell got to Scotland he was in for a surprising realization. He discovered that many of the problems he was passionate about learning to solve back home in Nigeria had already been solved in Scotland. The most pivotal memory for Mitchell was the problem of banking.

While Scotland had ATMs, debit cards, and direct deposit, Nigeria had no such infrastructure. In the early 2000s, banking in Nigeria was an arduous and stressful process. As Mitchell describes,

It was common to leave your offices, go to the banks, and collect tally numbers because you wanted to withdraw cash.

It was common for people to leave the office at noon and not return that day to work because there was a large queue at the bank.

It was common in those days for people to stack lots of cash on Fridays. Since the banks closed at four, Nigerians would go to the banks on Fridays to get as much money as you can for use over the weekend.

It was common in those days for you to be in traffic going home and you are robbed (at gunpoint) because there was a high likelihood that you had a lot of cash on you.

It was common in those days for you to be at home on the weekend and for you to be robbed (at gunpoint) at home because there was a high tendency that the robbers will find cash with you at home.[94]

Long lines, wads of cash, and robberies were a thing of the past in Scotland. At Schlumberger, Mitchell banked with an institution in the US, worked in the UK, utilized an international Visa card, and with the internet could do his banking remotely. The mix of homesickness and realization of how far Nigeria had to go was an inspiration for Mitchell.

After about three months, I left the job. I was being paid in dollars! And I left the job. I said, "I'm going back to Nigeria."

I said, "This still must stop!" I didn't have banking experience, never worked in a bank before, and had never done payments before. I was just an engineer doing networking. But I chose a problem that I could solve.[95]

Mitchell's hindsight of working in Nigeria, influenced by his short time working in Scotland, was the spark to create Interswitch. Just three years after leaving school and with no savings or family money, Mitchell was confident that his idea would beget funding and eventually success.

His goal was to create a cashless Nigeria.

INSIGHT

If you ask the wrong question, even if you get the correct answer, you've executed the wrong thing.[96]

To launch Interswitch, Mitchell started fundraising. His goal was 400 million Naira ($1 million USD).

Unfortunately, he was only able to raise 200 million Naira. Oof. Not a great start to what he hoped was going to be a global, world-changing business.

In the early days, Mitchell was extremely stingy. He counted the number of sugars that employees were drinking with their tea and cleaned his offices himself rather than hiring custodians. His pride fell to the wayside as he worked to execute on his insight. He laughs at the memory now: "It appears the way the world was made is that those that have good ideas, don't usually have money."[97]

Some of the early backers of his idea sat on his Board of Governors and included the CEOs of some of Africa's largest banks. During his first board meeting on December 4, 2002, the CEO of United Bank of Africa said to Mitchell, "We have invested in your company (and other companies). How do we know which one of you (compared to your competitors) will lead us to the promised land?" Mitchell, taken aback, realized that the question was an extremely important one: his idea to create a cashless society was not new. In fact, that same idea had been tried in Nigeria and failed countless times before.[98]

Sitting in his office after the meeting, Mitchell began to reflect. From the beginning, Mitchell had operated under the assumption that the improvement of Nigeria was synonymous to the removal of cash. "Cash is inefficient!" consultants would write in their reports. "Cash leads to corruption!" In spite of this universal recognition, no Nigerian FinTech startup in the early 2000s could effectively sell cash-eliminating services. Most focused on the point of sale and tried to create ways to use devices that would remove the need to exchange paper money. As Mitchell thought about his own experiences, he realized that just saying "cash is bad" was an over-simplification.

"No," Mitchell thought to himself. "Cash can't be the problem." Scratching his bald, black head behind his owl-y glasses, Mitchell asked himself the billion-dollar question: "Which country has eliminated cash? Maybe I can go to them and ask how they did it." He laughed to himself: *no* country anywhere had ever eliminated cash from their economy to become a "cashless" society, especially not in the early 2000s.[99] So why should Nigeria be the first?

Immediately I knew that trying to eliminate cash in Nigeria was a bloody waste of time. So how to redesign the question? The way to redesign the question was to look at my people. My people love cash! Why try to eliminate what people love? They need this for corruption—yes, seriously! They need it for parties, they need to spray (throwing money at brides and grooms at weddings or on coffins at funerals)! We love cash! So why eliminate what everybody loves? So out of this, I redefine the question that cash is not the problem: the problem is the way we use cash. Focus on how cash is used, and you will solve a problem.[100]

While everybody was trapped in the hamster wheel of attempting to eliminate cash, Mitchell arrived at a keen insight that would set his company up for a billion-dollar success where others had failed. "Nigerians need cash just-in-time." Nigerians needed cash in the right quantity whenever they needed it, instead of hoarding cash because they couldn't get it when they wanted it. *This* was the problem, not cash itself.[101]

And it's not just Nigeria that is addicted to cash. In fact, globally, as reported by the World Bank, approximately 40 percent of people do not have a bank account.[102] They are stuck with cash as a primary means of completing point-of-sale transactions. This is especially true of smaller transactions. As reported in the 2018 G4S World Cash Report, "In North America, over 50 percent of transactions under twenty-five dollars occurred with cash and over 60 percent of transactions under ten dollars occurred with cash." Despite the rise of financial technology, cash is king, and especially in 2002, cash was king.

This data was available for the world to see, but Mitchell's insight was in the fact that Nigeria's banking problem was a social problem rather than a financial problem. By reframing Interswitch, Mitchell found his niche.

Interswitch set out to create their own card standard focusing on debit cards to allow Nigerians to access their cash through ATMs whenever they needed it. No more waiting in long lines. No more stressing about robberies. Despite receiving harsh words and dissuasions of warning from existing international debit card manufacturers, the Interswitch team powered ahead.

Their business plan projected breaking even in four years. Mitchell's team did it in just two. Interswitch blew its competitors out of the water.[103]

Despite this continual success, 95 percent of Nigerians still used cash for payments in 2019. This façade of the "cashless economy" hasn't changed in the last twenty years; however, what has changed is the way in which people access their cash thanks, in large part, to Interswitch.[104] Today, Interswitch is a leading player in Nigeria's developing financial ecosystem with omni-channel capabilities across the payments value chain, processing over 500 million transactions per month.[105]

FORESIGHT

Think big, start small, scale fast.[106]

Mitchell's hindsight of his experiences in Scotland combined with the insight that cash is not the problem in Nigeria's cash-based economy, created the perfect storm for Interswitch. However, his foresight is what allows Interswitch to grow at an unprecedented, and almost unstoppable, rate.

So where is Interswitch going next? Mitchell smiles as he tells me:

Let me tell you a secret. Inter- means inter-connect: that was phase one, connecting banks. Inter-active, that was phase two; quick teller where people can transact. Inter-national: that is phase three. So, the "inter" is "Interconnect, Interact, and International.[107]

Today, Interswitch has a physical presence in Nigeria, Kenya, Uganda, and Gambia but sells its products in twenty-three

African countries.[108] Unsurprisingly, the company has plans to grow even further in 2021.[109]

Interswitch had big goals from day one and actualized on them from the one small office where Mitchell would stay late to clean. They have seen immense success in the last two decades, but one problem still plagues them to this day: brain drain.

I lose staff to Canada on a daily basis....The best brains are leaving this country and they are going to other countries. The only way out is for us to produce talent faster than we are losing it. Initially, I thought it was salary, money that was making them go to Canada: it's not...It's not about happiness with the company, it's not about pay, it's about quality of life... (The solution is to) produce more talent faster! It's clear to me right now that one of the products that Nigeria has to export is talent. The challenges are there but those challenges are creating opportunities for a new set of people to be gainfully employed. If one person leaves, somebody else has to replace them: it is our job to make sure that the person who replaces them has the skills and the knowledge to get the job done.[110]

Mitchell's opportunistic mindset is the crux of his foresight thinking: Where are there opportunities to invest today that will beget even greater returns tomorrow? For Interswitch operationally, this means focusing on developing home-grown talent, which Interswitch is doing by sponsoring Pan-African science competitions, hiring locally, and paying competitive global wages. Broadly, this work from Mitchell and other wealthy African entrepreneurs is paying off: according to a 2017 study by Jacana Partners, a pan-African private equity firm nearly 70 percent of African students pursuing MBAs at the top ten US and European schools plan to return home after graduation.[111] Perhaps even "brain drain" will be a thing of the past for Nigeria and the whole continent of Africa.

So, assuming you had unlimited money, which country would you *buy* to experience the greatest return in fifty years? Mitchell's success with Interswitch in Nigeria seems to be a positive signal of good things happening in West Africa. Especially when you consider that they have only captured 5 percent of the financial transactions market in Nigeria.

More broadly, however, the Interswitch Unicorn is a harbinger of what may be happening next in the rich and populous continent of Africa. Africa now has the fastest-growing middle class in the world with $1.4 trillion in consumer spending across the continent in 2015, according to data from McKinsey & Co.[112] By 2025, 65 percent of African households will be in the "discretionary spending" income bracket—defined as earning more than $5,000 a year. "Consequently, the profile of goods and services that Africans purchase will shift from basic necessities toward more discretionary products," the consultancy predicts. This along with the fact that Africa is the youngest continent in the world (with 60 percent of the population under twenty-five) is a perfect storm of opportunity.[113]

Through mindfully acknowledging hindsight, insight, and foresight, entrepreneurs in Africa and beyond will be able to mimic some of the successful characteristics that Mitchell used to confidently build Interswitch. These ways of seeing are the first step to asking the right questions, building the right solutions, and reaping benefits from the market.

The key to unlocking the Interswitch Unicorn lies in mastering the types of seeing that has led Mitchell Elegbe to defy odds as Africa's first African-founded FinTech Unicorn. Where others saw a dark continent, Mitchell saw light.

Chapter Summary

Lesson 1. Africa has become a frontier of venture capital investment and entrepreneurship with around ten Unicorn companies on the continent and more than $1 billion in startup funding deployed in 2019. Moreover, Africa has one of the fastest growing middle classes in the world with $1.4 trillion in consumer spending across the continent. Nigeria, as one of the youngest populations in the world, is leading Africa's technology startup revolution.

Lesson 2. Starting a startup often requires predicting future trends based on past experience (hindsight), seeing around corners (foresight), and reframing existing contexts (insight). Mitchell Elegbe utilized all three of these types of seeing when he set out to redesign the availability of "just-in-time" cash in Nigeria. In starting Interswitch, he reframed his startup's problems from being financial (eliminating cash) to social (removing the stressors associated with cash).

Lesson 3. "Brain drain" is a problem in Africa. Educated Africans often leave the continent to work somewhere else, like Europe or the United States. However, some entrepreneurs have found tactics for retaining the next generation of talent like hiring locally, training for a global marketplace, and paying competitive global wages to capture, train, and satisfy employees.

PART 2:

REFINEMENT

"Beware lest you lose the substance
by grasping at the shadow."

— A E S O P

Before returning to school for my sophomore year of college, I was thrust into the deep end.

I had just finished my summer internship at Twitter when my mother, the breadwinner of my family, took me to Red Robin's. "Michael," she started quietly as I bit into the crisp French fry, "I'm not going to be able to pay for your tuition." With tears in her eyes, she remorsefully walked me through our family's financial situation. With two older siblings in medical school, it seemed the only way for me to finish college was with debt.

And I wasn't alone.

As reported by Experian, in 2020 the total student loan debt in the US reached a record high of $1.57 trillion with an average student loan balance of $38,792. This ballooning number is a 12 percent increase from the year before. Like many Americans, while my Ghanaian immigrant parents had guided me to college, I now had to pay my own way. All my tuition: $45,000 over three years.

My head was underwater, and I didn't know how to swim.

When I walked on campus during my sophomore year, I realized that no on-campus job could provide me the money that I needed to pay tuition. Thus, I turned to entrepreneurship. After dozens of failed businesses (my *exploration* phase), I succeeded with the Enchiridion Corporation, a marketing consulting firm that connects talented low-income college students to paid consulting opportunities at local businesses.

Refinement was the moment that I started to tread water and got comfortable with what I was doing. I cut the fat and focused on the true value-add of my random ideas to my customers.

> *"My success, part of it certainly, is that I have focused in on a few things."*
>
> —BILL GATES

I went door-to-door in Harvard Square pitching my idea to businesses, creating legal contracts, and learning about the problems of these businesses. I had no idea what I was doing, but within three months of launching Enchiridion, I secured $50,000 of consulting contracts, hired twenty other low-income Harvard student employees to work for me, and incorporated as a Delaware S Corporation. As a result of my "little startup," I flew across the world to Shanghai, China and presented our work to the CEO of a $300-million restaurant chain, one of our clients.

With the profits made from Enchiridion and my summer internships, I was able to pay tuition without taking on debt. I even took a few celebratory vacations around the world to places like Florence, Italy and Mexico City, Mexico. However, the most rewarding memory was the fact that my employees were able to do the same.

Enchiridion was business as social justice, not business as usual. By starting with myself and retaining a heightened sense of social engagement and responsibility, I was able to create a positive ripple effect that changed the lives of those around me.

My business's name and mission were derived from the Greek word *Enchiridion,* which when translated, means "a book containing essential information on a subject." The next four founders that you will read about distilled their complex explorations into focused Enchiridions to develop mission-driven businesses. While the business world has infinite possibilities, these founders refined their visions to effectively pull along a team and create a focused impact.

First is Mudassir Sheikha who led the first Unicorn exit in the Middle East and North Africa (MENA) Region. He had an unyielding belief in his company, Careem, which stemmed from his belief in himself, the mission of his work, and the potential of the MENA ecosystem. As he scaled the business, this belief only became more refined.

Second is Cher Wang, the daughter of a billionaire who struck out on her own path to create HTC. Cher's life was a constant game of refocusing and reframing existing information and insights to derive new value. This skill enabled her to build a company that at its peak supplied almost 20 percent of the world's smartphones.

Third is the founding team of Andela: an eclectic team composed of two Nigerians, a Cameroonian, a Canadian, and two Americans who have built a business with the aim of making the African continent a technology skills hub. Crafting a $700 million company takes a village, even if its members are a collection of immigrants.

Fourth is Robin Li: the Chinese founder who cracked and patented PageRank search before anyone else in the world. Today, Robin's company Baidu is one of the top tech companies in Asia; however, it came about as a result of a variety of pivots and refinements to the initial strategy and insight that Robin had.

In their own way, each of these Unicorn founders were forced to develop into diamonds when put under pressure. After exploring a variety of possibilities, they refined their focus to core insights through believing, reframing, collaborating, or pivoting to eventually distill impacts that will outlast them.

"The successful warrior is the average man, with laser-like focus."

—BRUCE LEE

CHAPTER 4:

THE ABCS

What comes to mind when I show you this list of twenty-two countries: Algeria, Bahrain, Egypt, Iran, Iraq, Israel, Jordan, Kuwait, Lebanon, Libya, Mauritania, Morocco, Oman, Palestine, Qatar, Saudi Arabia, Sudan, Syria, Tunisia, Turkey, United Arab Emirates, and Yemen.

Perhaps you imagine desert heat in the setting of *Arabian Nights*?

Or maybe you think of the founding histories of world religions like Christianity, Judaism, and Islam?

Still others conjure up images of religious rivalries, repressive governments, or regional violence.[114]

I'll bet you didn't think of a robust startup ecosystem with Unicorn acquisitions, double digit growth, and new companies being born daily. The twenty-two countries above make up the Middle East and North Africa, or MENA for short. Since 2018, the MENA region has experienced exponential growth in the startup sector.

MENA is a region with extreme positives and negatives. In 2019 the region received $704 million in startup funding, and on March 26, 2019, it experienced its first ever Unicorn exit when Uber acquired Careem for $3.1 billion.[115] This, of course, all comes on the backdrop of existing statistics about the MENA region, which accounts for 6 percent of the world's population, 60 percent of the world's oil reserves, and 45 percent of the world's natural gas reserves.[116]

More broadly, the region is challenged with extremely high levels of youth unemployment and low female labor force participation. As reported by the International Monetary Fund, the youth unemployment rate in MENA exceeds that of any other region in the world at 25 percent.[117] Even more distressing is the female labor force participation rate, which is also the lowest in the world with only 21 percent of women contributing to the labor force and women contributing only 18 percent to MENA's overall GDP.[118]

Promoted by tailwinds like the growing startup ecosystem and discouraged by headwinds like inequitable unemployment and a weak technology infrastructure, Mudassir Sheikha founded Careem on the first day of Ramadan in 2012. With sleek black hair and genuine eyes that light up whenever he reveals his small welcoming smile, Mudassir has an aura of methodical thought that seems better suited for a consultant than a startup founder. That's not surprising considering the fact that he dabbled in consulting as an Associate Partner at McKinsey & Company for five years of his career. However, like every entrepreneur, he faced a problem that he deemed worth solving and left the established path to pursue an opportunity.

Since its founding, Careem has seen immense success. Sure, it was acquired by Uber as a Unicorn, but it also has over 600 million users in 15 countries and 120 cities including Egypt, Jordan, Pakistan, Saudi Arabia, Morocco, the UAE, Pakistan, Turkey, and Sudan.[119] They have created over 1 million jobs and connected cities, all while delivering on their mission "to simplify and improve the lives of people and build an awesome organization that inspires".[120]

Despite having a great idea, Mudassir's success with Careem was not predetermined. Nonetheless, by following his ABCs (Always Believing in Careem), Mudassir reveals a key lesson for creating a Unicorn company in tough startup environments like MENA. The story of Mudassir, and by extension Careem, is rooted in three types of belief, which have pushed the company to success: Mudassir's belief in himself, which inspired him to take risks, his employees' belief in Careem that inspired them to act as owners, and his belief in the ecosystem that has inspired cultural changes for the next generation of startup founders. Self, mission, and ecosystem are the driving keys of belief to unlocking the Careem Unicorn. Or, given the region, perhaps we call them the three-humped Careem Camel.

BELIEF IN SELF (RISK)

Every morning we would have assembly and Bishop Lobo would go up on stage to tell a story. I heard a story every day in my school years, and I don't remember many, but I remember one. The story was that life is like a boat with two oars. One oar is your hard work, and the other is prayers or blessings. If you just work hard and you don't have the blessings, then you're going to go around in circles. But if you simply keep on praying, hoping that great things will happen to you, you go around in circles as well. You actually need both of these things to push ahead. The story of Careem so far has been this story too.[121]

Mudassir grew up in Nanak Wara, a humble part of Karachi, Pakistan as the only son in a Muslim family.[122] His family shared an apartment that was across the street from a *Masjid* (a mosque) and every Friday, the masjid would open the loud-speaker to call the family to prayer. "I would tend to be the late-goer," Mudassir recalls with a chuckle.[123] Those weekly Friday prayers became a habit and heavily informed the environment that Mudassir grew up in. Even today, Mudassir constantly peppers his keynotes and interviews by saying "alhamdulillah," praise and thanks to God.

As a child, he attended school at Saint Peter's, Saint Michael's, and Saint Patrick's: catholic schools that were a departure from what he experienced at home. It was where he heard the stories and teachings of the Pakistani Bishop Anthony Lobo, which still inspire him today. These diverse experiences seeded in Mudassir a curiosity about the world and a love of education for its own sake. "My (favorite) childhood memories have been around doing well in school and being recognized by parents," he recalls.[124]

While there was always pressure to be at the top of his class, Mudassir didn't struggle. For him and his family, education was one of the most important pursuits. By the time he graduated high school in 1995, he received the best A-level grades in the country and was awarded a full scholarship to attend the University of Southern California, where he studied Economics and Computer Science.[125] By 2003, he had also received a Master's in Computer Science from Stanford.[126]

For the next five years, Mudassir stayed in California, creating startups in the aftermath of the dot com bubble. It was a lesson in building companies in markets that could sustain high-growth companies. "I lived in San Francisco," he recalls, "and every hundred meters there were billion-dollar businesses!".[127] After three startup experiences (two of which were exits), Mudassir moved closer to home in the UAE, with a bit of financial security, to work at McKinsey.[128]

After five years of working, Dominic Barton, a global managing partner at McKinsey, offered Mudassir the opportunity to create a new McKinsey office in Pakistan. Even though Pakistan was one of the biggest countries in the MENA region with over 200 million people, there was, up until that point, no McKinsey consulting presence in the country. "Since I was thinking of leaving anyways, I volunteered to go in and explore it".[129]

The exploration process was simple: Could McKinsey find enough high-value customers to justify the creation of a new office? Unfortunately, the results were extremely disappointing.

One of the things that we had to do was to make a list of clients that McKinsey could serve in Pakistan. McKinsey typically works with larger organizations, so we looked for larger companies. I was quite surprised to see that there was only one company in Pakistan at that time, which was worth more than a billion dollars. Pakistan is a nation of 200 million people. And there was only one company that was worth more than a billion dollars. Forget about the billion-dollar mark; that's irrelevant. But the fact that such a large nation of people has only produced one large corporate institution is a bit sad, a bit embarrassing as well. Why have we not been able to produce it?[130]

Of course, Mudassir admits, there were a few large oil and gas companies in the region, but the only home-grown non-resource Unicorn business on the Karachi Stock Exchange in 2012 was Engro, a multinational fertilizer manufacturer.

Spurred by this, Mudassir was determined to leave McKinsey and build an institution that could outlive him and have an impact as a billion-dollar business. He crossed paths with Magnus Olsson, a Swedish consultant working in the MENA region who was thinking of leaving McKinsey. As Magnus describes,

I had been in the Middle East since 2006 and really enjoyed what I was doing. But my life took a bit of a turn. I had brain bleeding out of nowhere (There was a chance I was going to die) and a very long story short, I survived, which was great. But it really gave me an opportunity to reflect on life....

While I was very happy at McKinsey, I realized that this is not my ultimate purpose. I need to do something really meaningful and big. So, I quit and went looking for that purpose. And in the process, me and Mudassir started chatting.[131]

Those discussions and the importance of creating *something* that was mission-driven led Mudassir and Magnus to ideate on what they wanted to create that could change the world. Oddly enough, they both left their jobs before they even had an idea. To them, all they wanted to do was meet two criteria: (1) create something with a huge potential and (2) create something with a social element to improve the MENA region and the lives of its people. For months they ideated on their codenamed Project Bamboo. "The idea was that bamboo you put in the ground, and then you water it," Magnus recalls. "For a very long time you don't see anything, and then it just goes up".[132]

The pair had a deep, deep sense of belief in themselves and that they could create something meaningful. And the worst that could happen? Well, as Mudassir described, if anything they would just look for a new job upon their return and the failed startup experience would have actually made them *more* valuable rather than less valuable.[133] The perceived risk of the startup was far lower than they had initially thought.

After exploring industries like health care, education, and even fish farming, Mudassir and Magnus settled on creating a startup focused on transportation and mobility. Their process was to identify problems and see if they could solve it with technology by talking to their potential end customers. Starting in Dubai, they realized that many of the taxi drivers living in Dubai were actually from Pakistan. Most of these drivers would move almost 1,000 miles away from their families to live in small, shared rooms at night then drive all day to make money.

We went and spoke to a captain (a Careem driver), and he basically said that he has three kids in Bangladesh, and he works sixteen hours a day. In Ramadan, he does three to four rides every day: that's it. Most of the time he's sitting idle and 90 percent of the money that he makes, he sends it back home to educate his kids and feed his family. He lives on 10 percent of that money in Dubai—in Abu Dhabi! At that time, the money basically gets spent on his bed, even though he doesn't have a dedicated bed. He shares the bed in multiple shifts with another captain. When we heard that story and we realized how difficult and uncertain it was for them to earn a living predictably, this is when the opportunity became meaningful to us. It's a big opportunity but it can also be super, super meaningful because we can make it easier for people like him to earn a living and feed their families.[134]

This, combined with the existing difficulties of business travel transportation in the region, made the decision to create Careem a no-brainer. The hope was to solve the problem of late pick-ups, paying with cash, haggling on prices, and even getting lost or arriving late to client meetings for business travelers. Imagine, they hypothesized, a world where business travelers land at the airport and hop in a pre-paid taxi to arrive at their client meetings on time. While a truism in Europe or the US, it simply did not exist in the MENA region.

Even with an idea in hand, there was still another hurdle to overcome: Mudassir's traditional Muslim family. Telling them that he was going to quit his stable job at a multinational company to start a taxi business was laughable. They were astounded. The same was true when Mudassir told his colleagues at McKinsey: even months after he left, they continued to call and ask when he would leave his taxi service to come back to his real job.[135] Despite criticism from family and colleagues, Mudassir's belief in himself prevailed.

On the first day of Ramadan in 2012, Mudassir and Magnus created Careem, inspired by the Arabic word *Kareem*, which loosely translates to generosity and is often used during Ramadan in the phrase *Ramadan Kareem* to mean "may Ramadan be generous to you".[136]

This intense belief in self despite ecosystem challenges, no prior examples, and pressure from family and work colleagues was the first ingredient in pushing Careem to success. More than just taking a risk, Mudassir's and Magnus' beliefs also inspired the creation of a culture-first and mission-first Careem.

BELIEF IN MISSION (CULTURE)

(When we started Careem) Mudassir came to my place in Abu Dhabi. The first thing we did was we sat down, and we wrote our values.... The first element is that we really want to do something meaningful, and we really want to be of service.... The second is this sort of crazy, ambitious "Let's shoot for the moon" type of notion. If you're going to do something, why do it smaller? And the third one is the idea of ownership. We want everyone to feel like a co-founder. Careem is theirs.

— MAGNUS OLSSON[137]

From the beginning, an intense sense of belief in the Careem mission was interwoven into the fabric of the company. It was clear to both Magnus and Mudassir that for Careem to succeed, they wouldn't just need any technical talent, they would specifically need technical talent that believed in what Careem was building. This same realization also stretched to the sorts of investors that Careem pulled into their journey of growth from the beginning and the methodology on which Careem was built.

The early days of Careem had to overcome two issues and each was rooted in the company's mission to simplify people's lives and develop transportation infrastructure. The first problem was acquiring talent, and the second problem was acquiring funding. Each was ultimately solved by convincing others that the self-belief Magnus and Mudassir had in Careem was not delusion, but instead was well-founded optimism.

They began by creating a business to offer transportation targeted at professional services organizations. For about a year, Careem focused purely on reliability, customer service, and integration with corporate portals to allow for convenient booking or information access for consultants, investment bankers, and other clients.[138] It was effectively a professional limousine service. Within the year Careem was generating significant traction and revenue.

As they continued to grow, they also began to hire talent. But they didn't look for employees, they searched for equity business partners who wanted to build Careem alongside them. As a result, employees at Careem are called "colleagues." Additionally, Mudassir and Magnus made the intentional decision to only hire individuals who fit within their aspired culture of service, aspiration, and ownership. Each interview tested for and asked questions to screen an individual's personality before hiring them. Even though it wasn't possible to have someone perfectly aligned, the goal was to hire individuals on broad strokes and bring them closer to the culture Careem hoped to build.[139]

While picky, this intentional choice to only hire those who aligned with the mission of Careem also had a tangible business benefit. According to a 2020 study by the Zeno group of eight thousand individuals across eight markets, "94 percent of consumers said it is important that the companies they engage with have a strong purpose, and 83 percent said companies should only earn a profit if they also deliver a positive impact".[140] This importance of purpose is also true for employees. In 2014, the *Harvard Business Review* found that "employees who derive meaning from their work report almost twice the job satisfaction and are three times more likely to stay with their organization to fuel business success".[141] All Careem's founders aligned on the importance of a mission-first company, and whether they knew it or not, a purpose-driven business is becoming an extremely important value-add for employees and consumers.

While talent and culture were Careem's biggest strengths, it was also where they made the most mistakes.

I think both the best things and the worst things (that have happened to Careem) have to be around the people and have to be around talent. That's the single most determining factor of success for us. The biggest mistake is probably getting people on board that are not aligned with the values and with the mission and then not making a decision fast enough to not have them in the organization. If you bring in people at an early stage, they're not aligned with what you want to build and the kind of culture that you want to build then that becomes the culture. They bring the culture, and they define the culture and very soon you have a lot of people that have been brought in by them that are not aligned with what you want to build…. We wanted some things done and we had to bring in people that were not fully aligned because they had the capability, but not making changes fast enough or recognizing the damage would be a mistake.[142]

Of course, given how picky they were, Careem was not always able to recruit talent. So, instead, they acquired talent. As early as 2014, they acquired a team from Saudi Arabia with the sole purpose of onboarding Abdulla Elyas and his employees as members of the Careem team. Even though it took a year to convince Abdulla, Mudassir and his team realized that talent was invaluable. This was a trend as Careem also acquired talent from Morocco and other locations. "Talent will pay for itself," Mudassir remarks, "so you should not be worried about paying for talent. These people will come in and make everything worth it".[143]

Mudassir also realized that having mission-driven investors was just as important as having high-quality, mission-driven colleagues. Unsurprisingly, Careem's first dollars in the business were all members of the "friends, family, and fools round." This ranged from prior colleagues at McKinsey to Mudassir's mother-in-law, but they all shared a trust in the founding team and a belief in the mission. A huge struggle was that most investors wanted to put their money abroad to diversify capital away from the unstable region of MENA.[144]

As Careem grew and proved to people the growth, need, and market-size, Mudassir kept the mission-driven investors on board. Uniquely, he recognized that many of these investors were some of the best, most well-connected people in the region. "If you have them on board as an investor," Mudassir rationalized, "let's get the most out of them by treating them like an extension of our team!".[145] He would give them home-work assignments and encourage them to lead sales, market-ing, or whatever their expertise area was with the intention of growing the pie to be larger for everyone. Specifically, these investors served as experts on financial contracting, opened doors to business development opportunities, and connected Careem's team to experts in the internet industry.

In all cases, the best investors and the ones who stuck with them were the ones who believed in the mission. More than being valuation sensitive and going with the Wall Street Banker who would give them the highest valuation, Mudas-sir reflects, it made more sense in the long term to get the right investors on board and ensure that the company will have the right chemistry with them.[146]

As Careem developed its employees and its investors, it also pivoted to grow its consumer base. Eventually Careem pivoted from a business-focused platform to a consumer platform. This optimism was rooted in the belief that their mission to simplify lives was one that could scale and become a better solution than their largest competitor at the time, Uber.

The learnings that we had building that business platform were the ones that really saved the day when global competition (like Uber) came into the market. The reliability that we had to hit for the business customer and the customer service that we had to hit for the business customer were really core standards that became our differentiators in the consumer space (When) competition came into the market, they had a service which had a better-looking app and they were giving a lot of subsidies to get people to use them, but they were not able to reliably get you from point A to point B...

The business platform that we had built with reliability and customer service really became the differentiator. The first round of funding gave us the ammunition to go and build a consumer play, show traction in the consumer play, and then raise money for the consumer play going forward.[147]

This pivot put Careem on the path to experience exponential growth and eventually to become the first acquired Unicorn company in MENA. Ultimately, a key differentiator for Careem was finding colleagues and investors who believed it was possible by believing in the mission of Careem to build an awe-inspiring organization.

BELIEF IN ECOSYSTEM (HABITS/INSPIRATION)

When we think about building an awesome organization, what does that mean? I think Mudassir has this inspirational vision of building an institution—an institution that actually produces world class parts and services, an institution that cares for the community, an institution that will outlast us and everybody else, an institution as a company that actually produces leaders.

—MAGNUS OLSSON[148]

In choosing to hire local talent, focus on local business problems, and battle local roadblocks, Mudassir implicitly doubled down on his belief of the MENA ecosystem. Even from day one, his aim has been to create a billion-dollar business in MENA. As he explains,

There are five thousand companies in the world that have been around for more than 200 years. But not a single one of them is from this (MENA) region.[149]

Careem's investment in local talent, products, and services has begun to change MENA both for consumers and future founders.

One of the biggest effects of having Careem in the region has been to create more gender equity for men and women. As Mudassir describes with a smile, "When we spoke to women, they would tell us about a pre-Careem Saudi and a post-Careem Saudi".[150] In the pre-Careem Saudi, women were not able to move around freely. If they wanted to go to the mall, run errands, or get to college, they were dependent upon their male relatives who could help them commute. This was especially true in the pre-2019 environment where Saudi Arabian women were not allowed to drive cars.[151] In the post-Careem Saudi, women were more empowered to be in control of their lives without a dependency on others.

This change also affected captains who were driving these women. Before Careem, it was almost unthinkable culturally for a Saudi man to be in the same car as a Saudi woman. For most Saudi men, the only time they were in close proximity to a woman was when they were near their sister, wife, or mother. Given how interesting these dynamics were, Careem invested even more heavily into the ecosystem by providing training to captains on how to interact with female passengers in Saudi Arabia.[152] Similarly in other regions, these trainings were a norm.[153]

As the laws changed, Careem changed as well. Being rooted in the desire to always "do the right thing," within thirty minutes of the announcement of Saudi Arabia's driving laws changing, a woman took the Careem oath to become a captain. The hope, Mudassir shares, is that "by 2020 we will have at least twenty thousand women captains".[154]

Of course, the uptake and cultural change has been quite difficult but there are stories that keep Mudassir optimistic given the cultural change across the MENA region and particularly in Egypt, Pakistan, and Jordan.

It's very humbling to hear the stories of some of these women who are working as captains. One woman that I personally met in Pakistan who was working for us had a husband who had passed away and she was responsible for three kids. Without having Careem as an opportunity, she was actually going and working in people's houses.... She didn't have any other options that would cover the expenses for her kids. But as soon as we launched the program where she could apply for a loan, get a loan, and purchase a car, she started driving.[155]

In addition to positively shaping female empowerment in the region through their belief in ecosystem change, Careem and Mudassir have also focused on creating employment opportunities throughout the region. Given the extremely high rates of youth unemployment, Mudassir beams as he describes how Careem creates anywhere from seventy thousand to eighty thousand new jobs every month across MENA.[156]

Ultimately, the goal of Careem is not to *disrupt* an ecosystem and grow through chaos. Instead, it is focused on *enabling* existing ecosystems to be more efficient.

Similar to other multinational startups like Grab in Southeast Asia (featured in Chapter 9 of this book), Careem is focusing on a long-term Superapp Platform with the hopes of making it easier to build any application on the back of its developed infrastructure. Mudassir's focus is on leapfrogging so that others don't have to pull all the basic building blocks together to create their next startup, but instead can piggy-back off what already exists in Careem's network. So, what's the bottleneck today? As Mudassir describes:

The region is not unified. It's not the United States of America. This region is made up of twenty, thirty countries, and it's quite challenging to operate in the region in a seamless way.
To build internet services like Careem,
You need certain building blocks.
You need credit cards.
You need payments.
You need last mile delivery.
You need messaging infrastructure.

You need good maps.
You need all these building blocks that don't necessarily exist in our region at the same level of quality as needed. So, what we (Careem) had to do in many cases, we had to build this infrastructure.... There's a huge opportunity to leapfrog.... We are trying to figure out what role we can play in bringing the cost of launching these services down.[157]

A Superapp vision would allow *any* founder to build on top of Careem in the same way that entrepreneurs can build on Squarespace, integrate with Plaid, or create detailed maps with Google Maps. In the long term, Mudassir hopes that his company can simplify people's lives so that they will have the mindshare, energy, and resources to pursue big innovation to create more billion-dollar startups in the region.

So, if Mudassir believed so much in the MENA region, in the Superapp philosophy, and in Careem, then why did he sell it to Uber? Oddly enough, the sale to Uber was also rooted in a deep believe in the MENA ecosystem. When Mudassir sold Careem to Uber, it was an event that created almost 300 millionaires for the employees who owned part of the company.[158] These are the people who will go out and start new enterprises, invest locally into growing the startup ecosystem, and create services to uplift the region as a whole. His idea was not to be selfish in taking the region's best talent, investors, and skills but to "sell-out" in order to free up the human capital for MENA to grow even further.

The path that Mudassir has blazed with Careem by believing in himself, the mission, and the MENA ecosystem has broken ground for future startup founders to see success. Even then as we look for more Unicorns or camels in MENA, a key to building these companies will need to revolve around a deep sense of these varying types of belief.

The key to unlocking the Careem Unicorn lies in taking risks by believing in self, building a culture by believing in mission, and inspiring others by believing in the ecosystem.

Chapter Summary

Lesson 1. Careem, the company profiled in this chapter, was
the first unicorn exit in the Middle East and North
Africa (MENA). The region accounts for 6 percent
of the world's population, received $704 million
in startup funding in 2019, and is the source of 60
percent of the world's oil reserves. Despite all this,
Mudassir Sheikha was shocked to discover that
Pakistan (one country in the MENA region) only
had one home-grown, non-resource billion-dollar company listed on the Karachi Stock Exchange.
Careem was created to change that while also having a positive social impact.

Lesson 2. Upon leaving their cushy jobs at McKinsey to start
Careem, neither Mudassir Sheikha nor Magnus Ols-
son had a business idea. They simply took a leap
of faith with the goal of creating something with a
huge potential and social element to improve the
MENA region. From a return perspective, this decision not only had social benefits but also helped
to attract more engaged and satisfied talent along
with customers who were more excited about the
Careem brand. Mudassir even extended this to
investors: giving them homework assignments to
help grow the business.

Lesson 3. Careem had a focus on everything local: local
talent, local products, local services, and developing a local entrepreneurship ecosystem. Even
with many avenues for independent growth ahead,

Mudassir and his executive team chose to sell Careem to Uber in order to feed talent back to where it came from. Ultimately, that exit created 300 millionaires and human capital for the MENA region to grow even further.

CHAPTER 5:

QUEEN OF REFRAMING

One of the first smartphones my family had was the HTC Droid Incredible. This five-ounce brick was revolutionary. Compared to today's paper-thin phones, it's an anvil, but at the time the credit card-sized device was a marvel. As a twelve-year-old, I was enthralled by the full keyboard that only revealed itself when you slid open the glowing touchscreen.

With a camera, built-in GPS, and classic Bluetooth it was, to me at the time, the best tech device since I received my Gameboy color. While my dad used it for calls, texts, or browsing the internet, I would use it religiously to play games whenever I was bored at church or in the car on rides home.

Now, close your eyes and try to imagine the founder of the company that built this phone.

Who do you think of?

Maybe you're imaging a black-turtle-necked Steve Jobs figure or an awkward Bill Gates. However, by this point in the book, you know that both of those images are probably not correct.

Despite the fact that millions of people around the world used (and still use) HTC phones, only a fraction know that the founder and brains behind HTC is Cher Wang, one of a handful of female billionaire tech titans. As the *New York Times* described in 2008, "She is one of the most powerful female executives in technology whom you have never heard of." Even if you had, maybe the croak in her voice or business suits would have thrown you off.

Cher has carved out a place for herself in the male-dominated worlds of both Taiwanese business and global technology. Perhaps in part due to the silver spoon she was born with, but primarily because of her penchant to reframe scenarios in uniquely Cher-like ways.

As the founder of VIA Technologies in 1987 and HTC in 1997, Cher Wang has defied the odds by breaking Taiwanese stereotypes and managing to multiply her family's already considerable wealth. While today 36 percent of entrepreneurs in Taiwan are female, when Cher started her first business there in 1987, it was orders of magnitude lower.[159] Even then, the use of one's family networks and influence did not guarantee success, especially as a woman. Cher, however, has achieved unicorn status both professionally and personally: becoming the richest woman in Taiwan and proving to be the most successful self-made child (female or male) of Wang Yung-Ching (Y. C. Wang).[160]

Cher grew up with two brothers and six sisters in one of Taiwan's most elite families. Her father, Y.C. Wang, built Formosa Plastics Group into Taiwan's biggest and most profitable manufacturing conglomerate. In its obituary on Y.C. in 2008, the *New York Times* described him as "the God of Management" who despite being Taiwan's "second-wealthiest person this year (2008), with a personal fortune estimated at $6.8 billion…is said to have lived an austere life."[161]

Being born into money, Cher should have taken a logical path: going into the family business and living off the multi-billion-dollar nest egg her father had created. But, as you'll learn in Cher's story, she is the queen of reframing. Rather than seeing her situation as a life-long windfall, she viewed it as a charge to develop her own success independent of family.

First, Cher failed in her dream of becoming a musician, which she reframed as a guiding life-philosophy of humility. Then, she abdicated her ancestral expectation and dove into the uneasy waters of entrepreneurship. Cher started her business with her own money (and a $180,000 mortgage from the home her mother had gifted her), reframing the risk as an endeavor for independence and innovation.

I never thought that my father would (financially) support me. I actually always was thinking about supporting myself because I really didn't have too much money in college and kept thinking "I really need to do something to support myself." I don't know why, maybe just the family structure and the traditions.[162]

Whatever the reason, Cher's success was dramatic, and at its peak, her company, HTC, was selling one of every six mobile phones in the United States. Understanding Cher Wang is a case study in understanding a "Queen of Reframing" and Cher's remarkable ability to look at old scenarios in a new light and ideate on entirely novel areas of value.

REFRAMING THROUGH HUMILITY

Growing up, Cher's family was "very strict." While other girls were learning how to become the ladies who lunch, Cher spent her leisure time playing tennis or basketball (two hobbies she still has with business associates to this day). "My father thought we should experience different things," she explained.[163]

Adding to the oddity of playing sports as a lady in Taiwan during the 1970s, Cher's father also espoused to her the importance of philanthropy. Every month, she and Y.C. Wang would take monthly visits to a local hospital that he helped finance. Rather than listening to The Beatles or Elton John in concert, her father insisted on staying humble, grounded, and thankful for the success they had received through hard work and seizing opportunity by giving back.[164]

Y.C. not only wanted to hand down money from generation to generation, but also his values of life. Surprisingly, this insight is a rare one even for wealthy families and undoubtedly contributed to some of Cher's long-term success. According to research from the Williams Group wealth consultancy, 70 percent of wealthy families lose their wealth by the second generation and 90 percent lose it by the third generation.[165] On the contrary, Cher has seen immense success, which in part has been the result of the lessons she learned from her father.

At the age of fifteen, Cher was sent to live with her sister in the United States. While some of her eight other siblings attended private schools in London, Cher opted to live with her sister in Los Angeles, and after her sister moved to Detroit, eventually enrolled in one of the best schools in Oakland, California, The College Preparatory School. She spent her senior year of high school away from everything Taiwanese and lived with the family of a Jewish pediatrician in Oakland.[166]

Despite being tens of thousands of miles away and surrounded by an entirely different culture, her father's influence still guided her:

I left Taiwan when I was very early (sic). My father actually wrote me letters almost every day. Sometimes one page, sometimes many pages. At that time, it was even before the fax machine so I could receive these long letters. We knew that he loves us. This is very important too to be able to communicate with your children and to really teach them your philosophy and your thinking. I think that influenced me a lot.[167]

These letters, which contained her father's thoughts on best business practices, were the distanced version of monthly trips to the local hospital that Cher had taken with her father growing up. They transported her from the comfort of her high school bedroom to Taiwan. It was 1974 and Barbra

Streisand's "The Way We Were" was the number one song on the radio all while the young Cher sat alone, digesting her father's letters.[168]

Unsurprisingly the lessons from these letters still stick with Cher to this day as she runs HTC.

After graduating from high school, Cher attended Berkeley with the plan to major in music and become a pianist. Alone and set to determine her own path, Cher dropped out of the program after just three weeks.

I think that playing piano actually is a good discipline for me. I even enjoy it today. I think the most important thing is the reality. If you actually go to a classroom, you may feel like all the students were actually playing piano and they could just play or compose the piece without any thinking. That's the difference in talent and think to yourself "I have to really stay home and study and go through it at night." I think the reality is just like business: we have to look for our weakness and strength.[169]

After failed auditions of Chopin pieces, a realization of her talents (or lack thereof), and a frank talk from her advisor, Cher shifted her focus to study economics, eventually receiving a master's degree in the subject.[170]

From childhood to her first bouts of independence in high school and college, Cher learned the value of using humility to reframe her position in society as a responsibility and to reframe her lack of talent as a reason to double-down on her existing strengths. The humility Cher exhibited early in her life persisted and is a key factor in the reframing mindset that allows Cher to internally direct her compass toward a more successful career as a businesswoman.

REFRAMING THROUGH STRUGGLE

"The difficulty lies, not in the new ideas, but in escaping the old ones."

—JOHN MAYNARD KEYNES[171]

Immediately after graduation, Cher fell back into the comfort of her family by working at First International Computer (FIC), a company founded by Charlene Wang (her sister) and Ming Chien (her brother-in-law).[172] After six years away as an independent college student and high school scholar, Cher reunited with her family.

Starting in 1982 at FIC, Cher was responsible for marketing and peddling the motherboard for personal computers to European customers. In her role as director of sales, she traveled around Europe while lugging forty-kilo hunks of metal and quickly experienced her first failure: a $700,000 scam. As described by Vincent Lo, Chairman of Shui On Holdings and friend of Cher Wang,

She made one sale of roughly 700,000 US dollars and that guy who had purchased something from her ran away to Spain. To Barcelona! Guess what? Cher pursued him and went to Barcelona with a bodyguard. She stayed there for six months trying to recover her money.[173]

That struggle was just one of the first that Cher had to overcome and hardened the perseverance she would need in her later business years. "We just had to solve the situation day by day," Cher reflects. "I think that perseverance is within ourselves. Everybody has it".[174]

In 1983, Cher led the launch of a new personal computer brand, Leo Computers. It was a year of excitement: IBM announced PCjr, Microsoft Windows was released to the world, and *TIME* magazine nominated the personal computer as the "machine of the year." It was the first time a non-human had ever been nominated.[175] Through Leo, Cher was at the forefront of innovation in technology. FIC quickly began dominating the nascent personal computer (PC) market and used the advantage of Taiwan's relatively low labor costs, large pools of well-trained engineers, and family connections to the Formosa Group's plastics to gain a major competitive edge and gain a share of the worldwide motherboard market.[176]

Eventually, however, the Leo project failed.

Cher was at the intersection of this fascinating market: FIC's Project Leo manufactured computers by assembling, branding, and reselling all the components necessary for a personal computer. Of course, that work was difficult: she had to engage with parts manufacturers from all around the world and this struggle was a headache. In classic Cher fashion, however, the struggle and failure were quickly reframed in her mind as an opportunity. While many struggle, few take these struggles and reframe them to create a company. Cher, however, dove right in.

When I started my first company, VIA technology, I was work-
ing in the motherboard industry. I was frustrated that we had
to buy all our chips from overseas. I believed that Taiwan could
design semiconductors too and could pack more features into
those tiny chips to save space. I found two friends in the indus-
try who agreed with me and so VIA came about.[177]

Realizing their unique position and opportunity, the trio
took a leap of faith and Wang left her sister's company to
cofound VIA Technologies, a Taiwan-based manufacturer
of motherboard chipsets, CPUs, and memory units.

The years leading up to founding VIA were defined by struggle: from the initial scam in Barcelona to the launch of a
failed personal computer project, Cher constantly reframed
her negative results as a potential positive outcome. A scam
became a way to practice perseverance and a botched product
became the flashlight to discover a gap in the market.

REFRAMING THROUGH CHANGE

"If you have a vision, no matter how difficult things are, it will
just become a process".[178]

Beginning in 1987, Cher ran VIA Technologies. She built up
an infrastructure in Taiwan to create and ship the hardware
that would enable companies like Apple, Microsoft, and Intel.
Eventually this even attracted attention from, and even a
conversation with, Andy Grove in 1992. Grove was the third
employee and third CEO of Intel, and in classic big-business
bullies small business, told Cher to "stop what you're doing"

since Intel was interested in the space. Cher scoffed and continued anyway:

What can you do? If I'm afraid of the difficulties, then I will never start anything, right? I think that it is important to really have a vision and just go for it.[179]

While Cher was physically working for VIA, her eyes were constantly watching the industry and her ears were listening to the chatter of the future. In 1996, she sensed that things were changing. Microsoft launched "Windows CE," which laid out Microsoft's vision for the future of mobile operating systems. The idea was to enable handheld PCs or small, portable tiny laptops that anyone could carry with them.[180] Hearing the news of this product launch and this vision brought Cher back to her days selling PCs in Europe:

When I was a young aspiring woman in my twenties, I was very enthusiastic and came to accomplish whatever was necessary—except I did not know how to direct this energy efficiently. All I knew is that I was very passionate; so passionate that I pushed myself into carrying a forty-kilogram desktop computer to demonstrate PC motherboard performance to customers all around Europe. I would drag these machines up and down the train because I could not afford a car. I can still remember all those bruises and sore muscles. When I set out on a train, I started daydreaming about a computer so small that you could fit it into my hand. A computer that could do anything as a calculator, a phone, or a self-organizer (I dreamed that) it would be so small and so light that you could carry it around easily. It was a silly idea at first but developed into a vision: a vision I kept in my heart for years.[181]

It wasn't until the broader market change in 1996 when Cher was able to take this vision and turn it into a reality. Sensing the change as the Queen of Reframing, she pitched the idea to H.T. Cho and Peter Cho in 1997. By the end of the year, High Technology Company (HTC) was born.[182]

By the time Cher had founded HTC, she was thirty-nine years old; decades after she initially had the idea for a phone that could fit in your pocket. While this may seem old, it is actually much more common than pop-culture would let on. As reported in a 2018 study with the Census Bureau and two MIT professors, the most successful entrepreneurs in any sector (including technology) tended to be middle-aged. "The researchers compiled a list of 2.7 million company founders who hired at least one employee between 2007 and 2014. The average startup founder was forty-five years old when he or she founded the most successful tech companies." Moreover, fifty-year-old entrepreneurs were almost twice as likely to start an extremely successful company as a thirty-year-old.[183]

With age and experience in her back pocket, Cher was in a position to build a successful company. In its early days, HTC started out building notebook computers. However, within months, Cher was approached by an old acquaintance at Microsoft who was searching for a manufacturer to build the handheld devices that Bill Gates had dreamed about integrating into the Windows CE Operating System. Cher was at a crossroads: continue making notebook computers or shift gears to the unproven, significantly smaller hand-held devices market. Cher's husband reflects: "HTC had strong engineers developing notebooks," said Mr. Chen.

"But it was a volatile business with lots of competitors. She saw that clearly and pushed for the other instead".[184]

The decision proved lucrative: HTC went on to make some of the world's first touch and wireless handheld devices and became a leader in the mobile phone and eventually smartphone businesses. Under Cher's leadership, the company created the first Android-supported phone; the first Windows-supported phone; and PDAs for companies like Compaq Aero, O2, T-Mobile, Orange, and Palm as a contract manufacturer.[185]

The path of HTC has been full of ups and downs (in 2007, HTC's revenue reached $3.7 billion but in 2020 stands at $210 million), but no matter the difficulty one consistency has been Cher Wang's penchant for reframing.[186] As an entrepreneur, her ability to view failure and weakness as humility, struggle as opportunity, and change as a reason to persevere has placed her in a position to thrive as a business leader. This skill, to reframe perhaps over-optimistically, is the key to unlocking the HTC Unicorn.

Chapter Summary

Lesson 1. Growing up rich does not guarantee that you or your kids will stay rich. In fact, according to research from the Williams Group wealth consultancy, 70 percent of wealthy families lose their wealth by the second generation, and 90 percent lose it by the third. Cher Wang, the founder of HTC, is not only an anomaly because she is one of few female Taiwanese business executives but also because she has materially increased her family's wealth by creating a startup instead of working for the family business as was expected.

Lesson 2. One of Cher Wang's key skills in founding HTC has been her ability to reframe problems in new ways by combining the information available to her. Working at VIA and seeing the growth of Windows CE, she was able to reframe her dream of portable computers into a reality by founding HTC and building micro-computers. Unsurprisingly, many billion-dollar startups are rooted in being a consumer of novel industry content and developing businesses before the broader market catches wind.

Lesson 3. Not every entrepreneur is born with the bug to create the next billion-dollar company. Cher, for instance, actually hoped to become a pianist until she realized that she was not as naturally talented as her peers. Late bloomers, however, still can achieve startup success. Cher was thirty-nine when she founded HTC, her breakout company. Researchers from the Census Bureau and MIT corroborate this anecdotal experience. In their study of 2.7 million companies, the average age of the most successful startup founders was forty-five.

CHAPTER 6:

IT TAKES A VILLAGE

It takes a village to raise a child.

From Igbo and Yoruba to Sukuma and Swahili, this timeless African proverb seems to be translated everywhere. It is probably one of the most popular, and cliché, cultural exports to the United States from the African continent. However, in reflecting on my own life, I see the truth of this eight-word quip.

Growing up, my village was composed of community members from the three churches I attended every Sunday, teachers or peers from school, and mentors who guided me to learn niche subjects. My village was distinctive because it featured a diverse, global perspective. My Korean piano teacher taught me the basics of Kaija Saariaho and Kimchi from her home. My Ghanaian grandmother taught me the importance of family and community service while raising me. My closest friends in high school showed me American, Mexican, Korean, and Vietnamese culture through lunchtime discussions. Sure, having a village matters, but what matters more is the quality of the surrounding village.

I was lucky.

Many of the founders in this book have been successful in part because of their own brilliance, but more importantly because of the brilliance and opportunities provided by their village. Community matters. The story of Cher Wang (Chapter 6). is a great example. Her father's influence and social connections were fundamental to the beginnings of the HTC story. Similarly, Hooi Ling Tan of Grab (Chapter 9). probably would not have seen success without the wealth, network, and influence of her co-founder, Anthony Tan. For individuals looking to break the mold, it takes a village to create meaningful change.

Even if you are a gifted child, your village is one of the main determinants of success.

In this chapter, I want to extend the claim one-step further. Just as raising a child takes a village, raising a company takes a village as well.

Generally, the village for building a company has a few major components: local talent supply near corporate headquarters, role models for potential founders, launch platforms (incubators, accelerators, etc.) to provide specialized learning, early-stage funding to grow from ideation, growth capital to hyperscale, and exits to refresh the talent pool with experience. Through repetition of this flywheel, villages around the world can create more billion-dollar companies. Slowly through a virtuous cycle, villages can become cities, known for their mutual value. For companies, the contributions to the village are called "the ecosystem."

Silicon Valley is perhaps the best example of a highly effective village ecosystem. These villagers specialize in minting high-growth, high-value technology companies. This village is so successful that if Silicon Valley were a country, it would be among the richest on Earth. With an output estimated to be $275 billion by the US Bureau of Economic Analysis, Silicon Valley has a GDP higher than Finland's.[187] So where in the world is the next startup village to match Silicon Valley's $128,308 per capita? Austin, Texas? Miami, Florida? Hangzhou, China?

Andela, a company with six cofounders, believes it will be somewhere in Africa. With hubs in Lagos (Nigeria), Nairobi (Kenya), Kigali (Rwanda), and Kampala (Uganda), Andela was founded around a mission that while brilliance is relatively evenly distributed across the human population, opportunity is not.[188]

This mission has taken the world by storm. Since inception in 2014, Andela has raised more than $180 million to fuel its vision of developing ecosystems and distributing opportunity. Its investors include Mark Zuckerberg's Chan Zuckerberg Initiative, Al Gore's Generation Investment Management, Google Ventures, Spark Capital, and more.[189] The excitement in Andela has been palpable, noticeable, and global. During Mark Zuckerberg's first ever visit to the African continent, he made a point to visit Andela's hub in Lagos. But why? What are these investors clamoring over?

Andela's business is simple. As described by CEO Jeremy Johnson, "It's like the Rhodes Scholarship meets Pivotal Labs".[190] The company invites citizens from around Africa to apply to join its fellowship, and after reviewing thousands of applicants, less than 1 percent are invited to join the Andela Fellowship. Becoming an "Andelan" provides access to one year of highly technical training from Andela and three years of consulting-like employment at a global company that needs specialized engineering services at an affordable cost. The goal of Andela is to connect Africa's budding tech ecosystem to the world. As Jeremy reflects, "We have become the primary pipeline connecting the technology ecosystems across Africa with the US".[191]

To date, the model has seen immense success. Andela has trained and hired more than 1,500 engineers across Nigeria, Kenya, Rwanda, and more.[192] In 2020, it began global expansion and currently has engineers from thirty-seven countries across Africa, Asia, Latin America, North America, and Europe. Andela serves more than 200 customers including Microsoft, Facebook, Google, GitHub, Viacom CBS, Coursera, and more.[193]

From inception, Andela has been built by and for a village. It took a village to develop individuals like Iyinoluwa Aboyeji, the mastermind behind Andela. It takes a village to create a training program that encourages students to attempt to (and successfully) give back. It will take a village to change global perceptions of a continent and demonstrate untapped potential.

The key to unlocking the Andela Unicorn is in the village.

VILLAGE OF SELF

Andela started in Lagos, Nigeria, in Mrs. Titi Adeoye's vacant duplex in 33c Cameron Road Ikoyi, which she handed us for free for our first two months.... The early days were really rocky, and we have a lot of people to thank for keeping us alive when it mattered most.... It is because of all of you, and many others, that we are here today.

—IYINOLUWA ABOYEJI.[194]

If I told you that two Nigerians, a Cameroonian, a Canadian, and two Americans walked into a bar, you probably would think it was the beginning of a bad joke. Not the beginning of a $700 million company. However, from the start, Andela has been focused on creating a diverse founding team to develop Africa as a technology hub.

One of the core co-founders of Andela is Iyinoluwa Aboyeji, or "E" for short. Born in Nigeria, E was the child of two pastors who were extremely involved in the Scripture Union Movement (SU movement) of the 1970s and 1980s. The movement's major doctrine was daily meetings to share the Christian gospel through the Bible and prayer.[195] E's parents were very involved in the movement and his father today leads the Foursquare Church in Nigeria, a global church with over 90,000 congregations and 8.8 million members.[196] This religious undertone guided E's life.

One of the stories that my parents told me was "What we heard from God when you were born was basically, I will reward your faithfulness to me by giving you a son who will become a glory for me to the rest of the Earth." That's kind of the prophetic quality that I operated under. It is really about how do you give glory and honor back to God. For all the amazing things that he does.[197]

The blessings have definitely come to fruition: at just thirty years old, E jokes that he is "retired" and is focusing the remainder of his life on giving back.[198]

Unsurprisingly, E attended Anglican primary school and Catholic secondary school. Even as a child he was attentive to business. Growing up, whenever family friends asked him what he wanted to be later in life, he would reply "A taxi driver!" E's childhood logic was simple. His father supplemented the family's income by "driving Kabu Kabu" (taxis) and at the end of each day, he would see the cash that his father brought home.[199] "I figured he was making a lot of money," E says with a boyish grin and slight chuckle that moved his whole belly. "All the money I could see was cash!"

Shortly, he discovered his second career choice: becoming a policeman. "I kind of noticed that the only person my father really gave that money to before he got home was the police!"

Chortling at the memory that is sure to be a topic of conversation at the Aboyeji household around family dinners, E recalls that he never lost his touch for cash. More than that, as E matured and embedded his religious childhood upbringing into his business philosophy, he realized the dilemma between personal success and collective success.

The harshest lesson I've had to learn, and I learned this lesson at the age of fourteen, is that personal success will not insulate you from the failures of your society.[200]

On December 10, 2005, when E was fourteen, he almost died. He was slated to board a plane with some of the brightest students in Nigeria from Abuja to Port Harcourt. He was going to school at Loyola Jesuit College and luckily did not board the two-hour-and-thirty-minute flight home. The *New York Times* describes the incident best:

Accident investigators sifted through the wreckage of a Nigerian airliner on Sunday, searching for the cause of a crash that killed 107, including dozens of schoolchildren heading home for the holidays.

That moment was a turning point for E: in a society with no emergency healthcare, fire ambulances, or hospitals, everything could be taken away. Individual success in Nigeria (or in any emerging economy) is like being a one-eyed man in a kingdom of the blind.

E graduated from Loyola, took a gap year after high school, and attended St. Jerome's University, another Catholic school, associated with the University of Waterloo where he studied Legal Studies and Economics. Throughout university, E was engaged in entrepreneurship. During his third year of university, he created "BookNeto," a startup designed to revolutionize education by combining easily accessed academic material with social networking and learning.[201] After working on the idea for two years, he sold the startup, packed up his life in Canada, and moved back home to Nigeria.[202]

I moved back home because there was a lot of work that had to be done to rebuild the country…. Most people tend to go the other way. People typically immigrate from Nigeria to Canada, not from Canada to Nigeria".[203]

However, E was confident that Nigeria would be the future. Perhaps it's best to hear the rest of the story directly from him as he blogged about it in 2016:

In 2013, Ian Carnevale, Nadayar Enegesi, Brice Nkengsa, and I started Fora, a distance learning platform for African universities. We reached out to Jeremy Johnson because of the similarities between his company at the time, 2U, and what we were hoping to build in Africa. We met at his office in NYC and then stayed in touch. From time to time, I would ask for feedback and he became my mentor.

In early 2014, it became clear that Fora wasn't working as we had hoped…. At this crossroad, we reached out to Jeremy again to ask for his advice. He had just gotten back from a trip to Nairobi to give a talk for the MasterCard Foundation. He had been invited out by Christina Sass, now one of Andela's co-founders, and while there, he started thinking of how one might scale high-quality education without charging tuition.

We met up at the Fresh and Co. on 28th and Park in NYC and I told him Fora wasn't working. We kicked around a few rough ideas and he walked me through one which would eventually become Andela. He promised to personally fund us and join our board if we were willing to consider it. I told Jeremy to give me twenty-four hours to think about it and talk to my team.

My team was intrigued and inspired by the model, though it was risky. Ultimately, Nad (one of my co-founders at Fora) convinced us that the new model was even more aligned with our mission to empower young Africans to take back the continent through education. The next day, we got on Skype and told Jeremy we were in.

Initially, we figured we would just try to pivot Fora as planned—we even ran the first recruitment and bootcamp as Fora. However, we quickly realized that Andela was actually a totally separate company, so we decided to start anew and wrap up Fora. Around the same time, Jeremy realized that he just couldn't stop thinking about Andela, and told us that if we were interested, he would leave 2U to co-found the company with us and lead it day-to-day.[204]

This was the formalized beginning of Andela. E and his team dissolved Fora, convinced Christina Sass to drop out of her PhD program at Harvard, and launched Andela with a global team of six co-founders.

What am I getting at? Andela is a story of people from all over the world coming together to solve a problem. This is one of our primary strengths as a company, and in part why we have attracted investments from great people like Zuckerberg. There would be no Andela without all these people—two Nigerians (myself and Nadayar), two Americans (Christina and Jeremy), one Canadian (Ian), and one Cameroonian (Brice)—making huge sacrifices to bring it to life.[205]

The team rented Mrs. Titi Adeoye's vacant duplex in 33c Cameron Road and began to build, fail, learn, pivot, and build once more. Andela was global from the start; incorporated in New York but focused on Pan-African solutions. It's no wonder the name Andela, is an homage to Nelson Mandela.[206]

While it is extremely positive that global founders and expatriates are creating local businesses, how does this affect local African ecosystems? Is the punchline of this story with six founders really a sick joke of resource extraction?

In a June 2017 study, Village Capital found that more than 90 percent of funding for East African startups went to expat founders and most early-stage investors in East Africa were expats themselves.[207] Viktoria Ventures, based out of Nairobi, found that only 6 percent of startups that received more than $1 million in 2019 in Kenya and East Africa were led by locals.[208]

Nigeria and South Africa fared a little better, with 55 percent and 56 percent raised by local founders respectively.[209] It's no wonder that locals accuse "wazungus," outsiders, of skewing the investment landscape in Africa. Consider the fact that African startups only raised $1.4 billion from venture capitalists in 2020.[210] For comparison, global venture investments in 2021 reached $125 billion.[211] On these estimates, less than 0.5 percent of venture dollars are going to native African founders.

Capital allocation aside, there also seems to be a much more predatory economic trend happening within Africa. In 2013, President Xi Jinping of China proposed the creation of a new Silk Road.[212] He called it "The Belt and Road Initiative," and it was an ambitious global infrastructure development structure to invest in seventy countries and international organizations to create new overland routes for road and rail transportation. It quickly received buy-in and investment from countries including Djibouti, Tonga, the Maldives, Kyrgyzstan, Cambodia, and more.

While a noble cause on the surface, many are suspicious of this initiative. In theory, if a country defaults on debt payments, China could claim the rights to a mine, a port, or money held in escrow. Given that China's banks negotiate and renegotiate sovereign loans bilaterally and in secret, they have leverage and can choose when to apply it.[213]

Could the belt and road initiative simply be a way for China to saddle countries with debt as a method of strategically gaining control of infrastructure? As Ian Roberts, a former managing director of Noozz.com, which specializes in emerging markets business intelligence, described to me on the phone, "This initiative has increased the debt-burden for already distressed economies and is akin to financial enslavement".[214] It's like a debt-strapped deal with the devil.

Is Andela depriving local African founders of funding? Are they simply the Belt and Road Initiative in new clothes?

To that, American-born of European descent Jeremy Johnson, Andela's co-founder and CEO, has a clear answer.

The reality is for the vast majority of our early investors we were their first exposure to the continent. Most of them have now made subsequent investments in Africa because of the comfort that they've gotten.... Our hope and expectation are that we will continue to see more and more funding coming into the continent and that we're going to be an example for investors around the world.[215]

Other Andela team members such as Seni Sulyman, the Global Operations Manager, has also added that in being a leader in Africa, Andela has demystified the fundraising network across Africa for all potential investors looking toward African startups.[216]

As one of less than a dozen Unicorn companies in Africa with a near-Unicorn valuation, there is scrutiny on Andela to not only extract value from Africa, but to return it to the continent as well.[217] However, at its core Andela has been successful because, unlike other investors or investment vehicles, their team is focused on developing the village rather than simply consuming from it.

THE VILLAGE COMMUNITY

If you're in the US and you're really talented you go to the Ivy Leagues.
If you're in India and you're really talented you go to the IIT.
If you're in China and you're really talented you go to top-tier universities.

In Nigeria, unfortunately, there is no meritocratic process for harnessing talent.
—IYINOLUWA ABOYEJI[218]

The Andela model is uniquely focused on providing Africa's brightest citizens with university-quality technology education that can be recognized on a global stage.

Starting in Nairobi, E, Jeremy, and the Andela team recognized three sides of the problem to be solved.

First, there was the local problem. Even though Nigeria's population was extremely young, there was no high-quality way to harness the talent of Nigerians (and other Africans) who couldn't find a job. "Imagine if you could teach those young people who try to scam people as a Nigerian prince how to make software. Imagine if you taught them business and how to channel their skill sets for good".[219] This, E argues, is an imperative in ensuring that by 2050 Lagos is thriving. When considered against the fact that by 2040 half of everyone graduating from high school on the planet will be African, there is a need to develop talent pipelines today.[220]

Andela is a platform that we built to raise the next generation of African technology leaders.... If you look at all the other developed societies, there are very clear meritocratic processes for allowing talented young people to fulfill their potential.[221]

Second, there was the global problem. Around the world, there is a technology skills shortage. Software developers are extremely hard to come by; even though they can get paid $120,000 a year or more. In fact, US labor statistics from 2020 estimate that "by the end of 2020, there will be 1.4 million unfilled CS jobs. Meanwhile, the number of graduates is only 400K a year".[222] The demand is so high that in the United States, software engineers have an unemployment rate of around 3 percent.[223] Globally, the numbers are just as bleak: McKinsey found that 87 percent of organizations are already experiencing a talent shortage or are expecting to face one within a few years. Essentially, if you're in software and don't have a job, it's by choice, not by force.

Third is a problem that has only been exacerbated during the COVID-19 pandemic. Seismic shifts in the market have changed the future of work, learning, and opportunity. Online education courses changed learning economies due to internet connectivity around the world. Moreover, as corporations and employees have been forced to stay home, there has been a marked increase in distributed work. While only 30 percent of companies utilized distributed work before the pandemic, post-pandemic it is projected that 48 percent of companies will have distributed workplaces.[224] Andela started under the operation assumption of 30 percent and has tapped into a green-field opportunity for growth.

A massive shortage of developers, increase in distributed work, and an opportunity to hire diverse teams beyond the twenty-mile radius of where companies normally looked: these unique insights were the birth of Andela. Their solution was to train high-talent Africans to contribute as global software developers. Allowing global corporations to distribute work and recruit beyond the arbitrary twenty-mile radius of location.

They started by building in Nigeria, a market with 168 million people and recruited their first class through Twitter. As described by Andela's president, Christina Sass, "We knew we were on to something".[225]

Unlike other re-skilling programs, Andela was focused on growing and cultivating talent locally. They did not require applicants to move and instead taught skills in Andela hubs located around Africa. Naturally, this battled the brain drain that tends to plague well-intentioned initiatives focused on training and development.

What made Andela truly special, however, was its rigorous application process. In 2016, they received 45,000 applicants to become an Andelan.[226] To narrow down this funnel, applicants are sent a logical reasoning problem-solving test to understand what kind of a problem solver they are. Andela learns about work styles, work ethic, drive, and aptitude to generate data about individuals. More interestingly, they refine what they look for based on how past, successful Andelans performed on the exact same test.

Next, they send the top applicants a test called "Proctor," which has been designed by the Andela engineering team to once again measure drive and abilities. After this, seventy-five are invited for an in-person interview to test for a values match and soft skills. Twenty-five are then recruited for a two-week boot camp where the Andela team tracks everything: how prospects incorporate feedback, how they contribute to the community, and how they learn technical content. The result? A 0.7 percent acceptance rate with six to eight people.[227] Even lower than Harvard.

As summarized by Jeremy Johnson,

What most people look for is where an individual is right now. They look for dots. Lines are way more interesting. What you want to look for is trajectory. How is someone growing and scaling and what is their narrative going to be? When you think about growth for a team member, you want to figure out who is going to be not just a great team member now, but who is going to continue growing with you and the organization especially for a high-growth company.[228]

Probably one of the most inspirational stories is that of an Andela security guard who was determined to become an Andela fellow. He applied repeatedly to the Lagos, Nigeria campus, learning more each time to snag one of the coveted spots.[229] Eventually, he was accepted. This security guard went from having no skills in computer science or technical training to becoming a master of over one thousand technical and soft skills that Andela teaches. Including a deep understanding of the EPIC core values of the organization: Excellence, Passion, Integrity, and Collaboration.

The Andela program is intentionally slated to end after four years. It's designed as an introduction into the global technology industry, not as a job forever. While the first year features training and internal problem solving, the last three years are a pairing between Andelans and host organizations that pay $50K per year for a high-quality developer as opposed to the $100K - $150K that they would traditionally pay for a developer in the global West.[230] Andelans are treated as regular employees: using native Slack integrations, traveling for two-week orientations in person to develop trust, and communicating regularly with team members through standups or meetings.

And the secret sauce? Because all Andelans are based in one of the Andela hubs, coordinating time-zones in Africa are strikingly similar to coordinating time-zones in Europe.[231] This pleasant surprise along with the high-quality of Andela engineers has worked wonders for the company's reputation and scalability.

There also is a return on hiring diverse candidates from Andela. As Jeremy Johnson reflects,

We as individuals, when trying to solve problems, see the world through the lens of our own experiences. No matter how broad those experiences are, it's kind of impossible for me to see the world through the lens of let's say a twenty-five-year-old young woman from Lagos, Nigeria. I can't do it! There are two ways that we can learn what we don't know (1) We can try and fail or (2) We can bring in folks who do have different experiences and who have gone through different life journeys.[232]

There is also a mounting business case on the importance of diversity. In a 2009 study conducted by Lois Joy, Nancy Carter, Harvey M. Wagner, and Sriram Narayanan, when Fortune-500 companies were ranked by the number of women directors on their boards "those in the highest quartile in 2009 reported a 42 percent greater return on sales and a 53 percent higher return on equity than the rest".[233] Another analysis of FTSE-listed boards found that operational performance and share process were both higher in the case of companies where women made up over 20 percent of board members than those with lower female representation.[234]

Andela is deeply aware of these statistics and boasts that 25 percent of their developers are women compared to 5.7 percent globally.[235] Whether caused by Andela's women-specific recruitment cycles or keen attentiveness to diversity, there is no denying that at Andela the benefit of the village community lies in part in its diverse perspectives.[236]

The village of Andela is small today, but in the next decade its lofty goal is to hire and train 100,000 developers around the world.[237] The Andela community is out to change the narrative.

EXPANDING THE VILLAGE

In many ways having a pretty strong mission orientation has actually been challenging.... The companies we work with don't work with us because they care about building the next generation of tech leaders around the world. That's not what they're trying to do. They have their own mission to solve.... We get to fulfill ours by ensuring that they are successful at theirs. Period.

—JEREMY JOHNSON[238]

Walking around the Andela office in the Nairobi campus truly feels like entering Silicon Valley. After entering the black Andela gates manned by security, visitors and employees are greeted by free coffee, nap rooms, whiteboards, soccer fields, video games, lunch twice a day in a cafeteria, and of course artwork modeled after Nelson Mandela. The only difference between a Google office and Andela's Kenya hub is diverse talent, which is unseen in the US where less than 3 percent of technology employees are black.[239]

However, as utopian as Andela is, every Andelan's journey comes to an end. Upon graduating, every Andelan is expected to contribute back to the development of the African technology ecosystem. As described by Christina Sass, this may take the form of entrepreneurship, scaling Andela as a member of the leadership, serving as an advisor to governments, or other forms of technology leadership within existing organizations.[240] The Andela stamp and network, then, becomes just as important as Harvard, Unit 8200, or Tsinghua University.

Some of the best examples of Andela alumni include two of the founders. In 2016, Iyinoluwa Aboyeji (E) left Andela to cofound Flutterwave, an integrated payments platform for Africans to make and accept payments from around the world. In March 2021, E's new company was valued at more than $1 billion.[241] Two of Africa's five Unicorns were started in the Andela family. A second co-founder to succeed in their post-Andela career was Nadayar Enegesi who left Andela in April 2021 to create Eden Life, a tech-enabled service to "put your chores on autopilot".[242]

Just like the PayPal Mafia, a group of former PayPal employees and founders, who created companies like Tesla, Inc., LinkedIn, Palantir Technologies, SpaceX, Affirm, Slide, Kiva, YouTube, Yelp, and Yammer, the "Andela Mafia" has generated billions of dollars of value already through startups like Flutterwave, Eden Life, TeenCode, Project Pink, and more.

The flywheel that Andela activates is only possible when talent, role models, incubators, funding, and exits feed on itself to expand the village beyond one hub to become a global movement. Rather than asking "What do you want to be when you grow up," Andela's mission is to force the future of Africa to ask, "What do we want to be when we grow up."

It is a sense of responsibility that says if my brother is down then I am down. It is a deep understanding of the idea that "I am because we are" (Ubuntu).[243]

As a Ghanaian American, I find the Andela model fascinating. When I first learned computer science, it was in a model much like the Andela model. Microsoft employees commuted every morning to my high school in the suburbs where I learned computer science surrounded by peers from all over the world (Korean, Indian, German, American, and more) from two professors who had also immigrated to the United States. In the digital village of ones and zeros, Andela's strategy of activating a village becomes even more global and international. I've experienced it, and it's a future worth living in. The key to unlocking the Andela Unicorn is in the village.

Chapter Summary

Lesson 1. If Silicon Valley were a country, it would be one of the richest on Earth with a GDP higher than Finland. Andela is built on the belief that an African hub may be the next Silicon Valley. They run a fellowship that provides access to one year of technical training and three years of consulting to connect Africa to the rest of the US while also developing a talent ecosystem in its African hubs. This model is hyper-localized and can be a blueprint for entrepreneurs hoping to start enterprises as an expatriate in a country where they're not from.

Lesson 2. Andela's founding team is extremely diverse: composed of two Nigerians, a Cameroonian, a Canadian, and two Americans. What's troubling, however, is that this is part of a larger trend of expat founders in Africa. Village Capital found that 90 percent of funding for East African startups went to expats and only 6 percent of startups that received more than $1 million in East Africa were led by locals. While one of the major founders of Andela is Iyinoluwa Aboyeji ("E"), only 0.5 percent of venture dollars annually are going to native African founders. With the limited amount of venture dollars available in Africa, Andela walks a fine line between depriving African founders of funding and opening the eyes of hesitant investors to an entirely new ecosystem.

Lesson 3. A 2009 study found that Fortune 500 companies with women on their boards reported 42 percent greater returns in sales and 53 percent higher returns on equity than comparable companies. Andela is deeply aware of this and explicitly recruits, hires, and staffs diverse talent (both in race and gender) to diversify the development ecosystem while also providing higher returns.

CHAPTER 7:

PIVOT PLAYER

———

Robin Li is an unassuming man. He is below-average height at a whopping five feet and five inches. If you looked at him, you'd probably miss him. His floppy, straight black hair, slacks, and belt to match his shoes make him look more like an eager intern than a tech CEO.

But that's just the way he likes it.

As Robin explains,

I'm an engineer by training. I think every entrepreneur is different: for me, I don't want to be recognized on the street wherever I go…. I enjoy life like ordinary people. But, because of my background I'm very excited about the possibilities that technology can bring to the world.[244]

A low-key statement from a man who created Baidu, China's largest search engine with more than 316 million monthly active users, about the population of the United States.[245]

Growing up Robin seemed just as unassuming. Born in November 1968 as *Lǐ Yànhóng* in the Yangquan Shanxi Province region of China, "Robin" grew up in a seven-member household. His parents were factory workers who worked daily to support their four daughters and one son (Robin). He wasn't born with a golden spoon. Despite the oppression that surrounded him, Robin was always able to focus on stamp collecting, performing traditional opera, and other interests including, eventually, computers.[246]

He worked hard and eventually followed in the footsteps of his older sister to attend Peking University, the "Yale" of China. Unsurprising in retrospect, he studied Information Management.[247]

Robin's undergraduate experience was in the midst of China's cultural revolution. While he was bright enough to study at one of Beijing's finest universities, he couldn't avoid the government's crackdowns that followed the pro-democracy demonstrations in Tiananmen Square. In 1989, as a sophomore, Peking University was shut down. The experience inspired him to study abroad.[248]

China was a depressing place, I thought there was no hope.[249]

After graduation, Robin applied to the top three graduate programs in computer science in America but did not get into any of them (perhaps, he says, because China was considered an also-ran in technology). He "blindly sent out twenty applications…SUNY Buffalo was the only program willing to give me a fellowship." In 1991, Robin moved to New York and attended The SUNY at Buffalo as a PhD student in computer science.[250]

Less than three years later, Robin pivoted. He dropped out of the program, received a master's degree in 1994, and began his life in industry.

Robin Li is a master of "the pivot." From pivoting industries, to pivoting jobs, to pivoting strategies, he is a case study in what it means to be a pivot player.

But is pivoting even important?

A study from Station F, a Parisian business incubator, estimates that nearly 80 percent of small firms make some sort of daring change or pivot during their existence.[251] During times of extreme strain like a financial crisis or global pandemic, these numbers are even higher. Even though a pivot seems simple (all you're doing is shifting business strategies to test a new startup approach after receiving direct or indirect feedback), academics argue that there may be at least eleven different types of pivots for software and non-software startups.[252] From zoom-in pivots to customer segment pivots to business architecture pivots, the ability to fail fast and iterate to avoid failure in the future is a skill required of every entrepreneur.

The key to unlocking Robin Li and the Baidu Unicorn is in understanding the art of the pivot.

PIVOTING INDUSTRIES

After receiving his master's degree, Robin began confronting one of the time's biggest technical problems: sorting information. While Sergey Brin and Larry Page (Google's founders) were getting PhDs at Stanford, Robin worked at IDD Information Services, a New Jersey division of Dow Jones & Company. There, he helped develop software programs for the *Wall Street Journal*'s online edition and created real-time information systems for Wall Street firms.[253]

But in his free time, Robin spent much of his days trying to solve the information sorting problem. On both coasts, computer geeks were racing to crack a multi-trillion-dollar nut.

Eventually, Robin did it.

While working for Dow Jones, he created and patented the algorithm that inspired Google and powers Baidu to this day: RankDex.[254] RankDex was the first web search engine that used the number of hyperlinks to determine the importance of web pages and check the quality of a website rather than search keywords.[255] The innovation, which seems like a no-brainer now, was ground-breaking at the time.

It was 1996. Two years before Larry Page patented PageRank (a similar algorithm that used link analysis) and started Google, with a reference to RankDex in their legendary patent.[256]

The moment I created this thing I was very excited, Robin recounts. I told my boss (at IDD) and pushed him. But he wasn't very excited. He told me "That's not what we do here".[257]

Despite holding the keys to the kingdom, Robin didn't pivot to the startup world. Instead, he continued to advertise his findings to technology companies and individuals at computing conferences and in conversations.

During one of these computer conferences, Robin set up a booth to demonstrate his search findings and met William Chang of a small startup named "Infoseek." After just one conversation, he was recruited to work on search development. As Chang describes in retrospect, "Robin is possibly the single most brilliant and focused person I know. And his inventions, now widely adopted, are still the gold standards in Web search relevance".[258]

Like the maestro he is, Robin pivoted to work at Infoseek.

PIVOTING JOBS

The Sapphire case is on the evening of the night,
and the flowers are scattered and the stars are raining.
The BMW Carving Car is full of roads.
The sound of the phoenix sounds, the jade pot turns,
and the dragon dances for a night.
The moth snow willow gold, the laughter is full of fragrant incense.
People look for him thousands of Baidu.
When I look back, the man is there, and the lights are dim.[259]

He joined in July 1997 and received $45,000 a year to think up algorithms. Living in Silicon Valley, he rubbed shoulders with some of the greats including Jerry Yang, the co-founder of Yahoo, and John Wu, the then head of Yahoo's search engine team.[260] Both were a connection from thirty-four-year-old biochemist and Robin's eventual Baidu co-founder, Eric Xu. During his time there, Robin developed more search functions including image-based search algorithms.

So why isn't Infoseek or Go.com the company that everyone uses to search online? Eventually, due to a controlling investment by Disney, Infoseek shifted its focus from search to content.[261]

Frustrated by the move, Robin and Eric ideated on a way out. After a conversation with Yahoo's search team at a picnic in the summer of 1998, Robin realized that all the major players were underestimating search and focusing on content. John Wu recalls the conversation:

The people at Yahoo didn't think search was all that important, and so neither did I. But Robin seemed very determined to stick with it. And you have to admire what he accomplished.[262]

One picnic was the pin that pushed Robin's pivot forward. Robin, in the face of pessimism, was unfazed. Less than a year later, he left to create his own internet company.

I am a very dedicated person. Once I've made up my mind about something, I will not change. I will keep doing it until it's better and better.[263]

At that moment, Robin was no longer an engineer: he was a founder.

With Eric Xu, Robin launched "Baidu," a name which comes from a poem written more than 800 years ago during China's Song Dynasty.

The poem compares the search for a retreating beauty amid chaotic glamour with the search for one's dreams while confronted by life's many obstacles. "...Hundreds and thousands of times, for her I searched in chaos / Suddenly, I turned by chance, to where the lights were waning, and there she stood." Baidu, whose literal meaning is "hundreds of times," represents a persistent search for the ideal.[264]

Or, in other terms, a poem about the art of the pivot and finding light in a perfectly timed change of direction.

Eric and Robin presented their business plan in the Bay Area and managed to raise $1.2 million from venture capitalists like Bob King, Greg Penner, Scott Walchek, and Hugo Shong. Nine months later, in September 2000, two other venture capital firms, Draper Fisher Jurvetson and IDG Technology Venture, pumped another $10 million into the startup despite only having twenty employees.[265] Within the year, Robin had incorporated Baidu and set up shop in Beijing to build the future of search.[266]

"When I came back I was prepared for a rough life. It turns out it wasn't so bad."

They began by offering search services to other Chinese portals rather than a stand-alone search engine. With $12 million in the bank, their main goal was to prove out this business model.

When we started Baidu, the business model was to provide the back-end search technology for internet portal companies in China. We did that and came up with very good Chinese search engine technology. Then we signed up a lot of the Chinese portals in a very short period of time: Sina, NetEase and

Sohu, Yahoo China, and any major portal company you can think of in China. What we quickly found was that we were still losing money. Although we signed up the portal companies that accounted for 80 percent of search traffic, Baidu still could not survive.[267]

Robin quickly realized that they were too optimistic about internet growth in China and couldn't create a business model predicated on picking off pennies from the big guys. Even with 80 percent of all Chinese internet users on Baidu (which at the time wasn't much, considering how there were only ten million internet users), Baidu's business model was not built to succeed. While they needed large contracts to sustain growth, internet portal companies were focused on buying the cheapest technology, not the best technology. This made Baidu's business extremely hard.

It required a pivot to different technologies.

Many of Baidu's board of directors opposed the shift. They worried that it would turn customers into competitors.[268] Robin was adamant that it was the right move and pointed to the success of Overture—a company in Pasadena, California, that sold advertising space correlated with search results (which meant, for example, that ads for dental clinics might pop up next to search results for cavities)—as evidence of success.

In the summer of 2001, Robin and the team switched gears to pivot from being a back-end technology provider to front-end consumer service. They mocked up a no-frills home page and on September 20, 2001, Baidu.com went live.

We were skeptical about search," says Scott Walchek, a part-ner at Integrity Partners and a member of Baidu's board. "But we weren't as smart as Robin. Robin said he had a unique opportunity to build a brand around search. And he was right.[269]

But at the time, not even Robin knew if the pivot was the right decision to make. The uncertainty pushed Robin to make his third pivot and launched him and Baidu into the Unicorn status it has today.

PIVOTING ROLES

Unlike a back-end service, which was more of a commodity, creating a front-end search platform required a heavy lift of engineering: design, user experience, product engineering, and more. Not to mention the fact that other Chinese search brands had years of experience and reputation with the Chinese public when compared to Baidu.

"It was a significant move for Baidu to change in 2001 from a search service provider for portals to a search engine facing direct-end users," Robin reflects.[270]

I realized that our technology was not as good. So, I went back to engineering and told them that:

We need to work harder. I'm no longer your CEO, consider me as your product manager. You engineers are used to coming to the office at 10 a.m. but starting from today you need to come at 9 a.m. to have a meeting with me."

I was holding meetings twice a day with engineers to push them to move faster and come out with better quality search services. I did that for about ten months, and that's what helped us to create better search technology.[271]

Like the Pivot Player he is, Robin decided to pivot *himself* in addition to pivoting the organization to truly push Baidu over the edge when compared to the competition. Within months, Baidu was innovating in the space: allowing advertisers to bid for ad space and pay Baidu every time a customer clicked on an ad even before Google created this model of doing business. And by the end of 2001, Robin's pivot was deemed a success, and he was named one of the top ten Chinese Innovative Pioneers.[272]

Small and medium-sized companies loved it, the site became deluged with traffic, and Baidu turned a profit in 2004. They even raised eyebrows from Larry Page and Sergey Brin of Google who, in 2004, invested $5 million into the company (after previously investing $10 million).[273]

When we realized that what we really were good at was search, we started to innovate to come up with all kinds of features to attract Chinese internet users. We really needed to innovate and evolve. When I gave up the CEO job and functioned as the Engineering Manager with Project Gleason we really wanted to catch up. Once you find out what you should do, you need to stay focused. Back in 2001–2002, many people thought search was a done-deal and that it was boring and figured out in terms of technology and product. But we thought we could do a better job and resisted all sorts of temptations to be a portal, an

SMS player, do online game development, and other things to really, really focus on Chinese search. That's how we got here.[274]

On August 5, 2005, Robin made the final pivot: from the child of factory workers in a seven-person household to becoming a Unicorn.

Baidu IPO'd on the NASDAQ, and in its first day of trading shares exploded from $27 to $122. It was the first Chinese company to be included in the NASDAQ-100 Index, was up 354.85 percent, and achieved the best performance for a foreign company listed on NASDAQ since the dotcom peak in 2000.[275] The event was huge financially and contributed to the branding of Baidu which quickly became known as "China's Google".[276]

Today, Baidu has a market value of $47 billion and operates the fourth-most trafficked website in the world.[277] Robin Li is worth $10 billion.

The key to unlocking the Baidu Unicorn and Robin's success is not in its product, but in its pivots. Robin's first pivot to switch industries from research, his second pivot to work in search, and his third pivot to return to engineering to grow Baidu in a new market are examples of the non-operational insights that are required to generate outsized returns. A summary of Baidu's expertise requires looking no further than the poem that inspired its name:

Suddenly, I turned by chance, to where the lights were waning, and there she (Baidu) stood.

Chapter Summary

Lesson 1. Eighty percent of small firms make some sort of daring change or pivot during their existence. Whether caused by a financial crisis or global pandemic, the ability to shift business strategies to test a new startup approach after receiving feedback is a necessary skill that Robin Li demonstrated through his life, career, and education. At Baidu specifically, their team pivoted business models and target market to immense success.

Lesson 2. Generally, the world of startups is small. Robin Li, while founding Baidu, rubbed shoulders with a variety of successful startup founders including Jerry Yang (the co-founder of Yahoo) and John Wu (Yahoo's search engine team). This cross-pollination of expertise and ideas helped to inform the pivots that Robin eventually took while creating companies and leaving his corporate job. In fact, the co-founders that Robin created Baidu with he met by chance at events like picnics.

Lesson 3. A business model is just as important as a product itself. You can have the best technology, but until you discover the right way to sell, success will be nearly impossible. At Baidu, this involved shifting focus from being a back-end technology provider to front-end consumer service. With this business model change, Baidu also re-invented their product to great success. Entrepreneurs building businesses should be willing to experiment; rarely is the first option tried the "right" option.

PART 3:

EXECUTION

"Ideas are a commodity. Execution of them is not."

—MICHAEL DELL

When I got my first corporate job at Microsoft, I felt my creativity dying.

In college creativity was easy: every experience was new. New people, new classes, new professors, new philosophies, new, well, everything. The newness forced me to reconcile with myself and one of the only ways to understand this was to write. But work was simple in comparison. The days were scheduled, meetings were prepared, and a majority of energy was spent on *execution,* not *exploration*. As I looked back, my journal entries took a different turn: becoming logs and databases rather than lyrics and dances.

As the months wore on, I realized the crux of the problem. In college, everything I did was for myself. I woke up for class not because I needed to, but because I wanted to. I was excited to attend a lecture on the history of Picasso from 1910–1914 or ecstatic to learn about Shoshana Zuboff's concept of surveillance capitalism. This bled into every aspect of my life: my life was, objectively, my choice. The office was different. Especially as a new employee, my success was measured by how accurately I could achieve someone else's goals. A promotion was based on making my manager's job easier and a "successful" project wasn't based on my opinions, but on the opinions of the all-knowing "customer."

So how does one execute on being creative in such an environment? Peer pressure.

"It's perfect," I rationalized. "I'll write my thoughts online and ask my friends to subscribe. Then if I don't write every day, they can hold me accountable for failing to hold up my end of my deal with myself." Finding a topic wasn't hard: "If I want to become a successful startup founder and every startup begins with an idea, I'll write one startup a day for a year then take one of those to make a business." Simple enough, right?

On November 14, 2019, I began the experiment and launched my blog: BillionDollarStartupIdeas.com. I published my first post at 7:34 a.m. while sitting in my childhood bedroom. In retrospect it was the domino that started a global movement.

Today, my blog has nearly 1 million page views, 75,000 readers in more than 175 countries, and thousands of replays on TikTok.

"Having a vision for what you want is not enough. Vision without execution is hallucination."

—THOMAS A. EDISON

Through my blog, I posted every day, religiously: giving myself requirements like "You can't eat lunch until you post" or "You can't take a shower until you write." At times, I scoffed at my own rules, but I knew that the worst thing I could do was to miss two days in a row. The Squarespace analytics tab became my addiction. Every day, my stomach would warm as I waited for the three buffering dots to reveal my prize for the day: the number of unique viewers and page views.

It was a game. My only goal was to beat my high score from the day before. My daily newsletter became a way for me to stand on a soapbox to the true fans who supported and admired what I did. It showed me that my thoughts, my notebooks, had value.

The next three founders that you will read about all had similar addictions. The key learning to scaling a business once you've explored a variety of possibilities and refined into a focus area is to execute relentlessly. Even after selecting an idea and refining it, success is a direct result of executing on a strategy.

First is Ritesh Agarwal, India's youngest billionaire and the founder of OYO Rooms, the fastest growing hotel chain in the world. Ritesh, while smart, shot above his peers due to an ambition-led execution style, which pushed him to minimize regret, expand his world view, and trickle down his goals to his employees.

Second is Hooi Ling Tan, the co-founder of Grab, a $10 billion Southeast Asian transportation company and Superapp. Operating in over 350 cities across a variety of government jurisdictions, Hooi Ling's strategy for growth relied on partnerships with an unlikely co-founder, local taxi drivers, and strategic government business partners.

Third is Bang Si-Hyuk, the mastermind behind BTS, the world-renowned South Korean K-Pop idol boy band with three number one Billboard albums in 2020 (the same number as The Beatles). Considering how the group sings primarily in Korean, Bang defied the odds with an execution strategy that relied heavily on social media and exploiting content-market fit to break into a global music market.

Each of these Unicorn founders offers valuable insights into the types of relentless execution that is required for a refined idea to become a full-fledged business. They aren't daily bloggers like me, but the daily interactions and learnings they've had from their businesses are examples of the many ways that startup founders can generate enthusiasm about an idea.

> *"To me, ideas are worth nothing unless executed. They are just a multiplier. Execution is worth millions."*
>
> —STEVE JOBS

CHAPTER 8:

STRATEGIC AMBITIONS

———

India has 137 billionaires. The youngest is a twenty-seven-year-old college drop-out.[278] He's younger than Snapchat's founder, Evan Spiegel, and richer than mega-celebrity Kylie Jenner, but almost no Americans know his name.

Almost is the key word.

There's one American who's quite familiar with this young billionaire's work. While visiting India in February 2020, former real estate mogul and US President Donald Trump remarked "You are a brilliant businessman...I actually know your company. Good job."[279]

This no-name made his money by creating the fastest-growing hotel company in the world in 2013, OYO Rooms (or OYO for short). Since then, the company has seen immense success. In 2019, its revenues soared to $951 million with over 25,000 direct employees (or OYOpreneurs), nearly 1,200,000 rooms across the globe, and 44,000 properties under management. For context, Marriott, one of the world's largest and most recognizable hotel chains, was started in 1927, made $20 billion in revenue in 2019 and only has 1,380,000 rooms globally in 7,350 properties under management.[280]

OYO's revenue, employment, and scale numbers are phenomenal, especially given the company's age, but it doesn't stop there: in 2019, OYO hosted over 180 million guests (on average 750,000 guests per night) with satisfaction ratings of 7.5+/10. Customers love OYO and their app is among the top three hotel booking apps globally with 2.3 million downloads per month, accounting for more than 90 million total users.[281] A darling of the public, *The Economic Times* named OYO its "2018 Startup of the Year" and investors like SoftBank, Sequoia Capital, and Lightspeed Venture Partners value OYO at more than $10 billion.[282]

But seven years ago, OYO didn't exist.

Where did this company come from? Who is the young prodigy that Donald Trump admires? And how did he do it?

His name is Ritesh Agarwal, and he is a case study in strategic ambition. Through minimizing regret, expanding world views, and fostering trickling down inspiration, Ritesh created the conditions for OYO to become the fastest growing hotel chain in the world.

MINIMIZING REGRET

Whenever I have two opportunities, risking it versus regretting it, I will always invariably choose risking it because I will never want to regret that I did not pursue something that I really want to do.[283]

I like to think that Ritesh Agarwal became an entrepreneur by chance. Born in Bissam Cuttack and raised in the southern half of the Indian Odisha state, Ritesh grew up in an environment where more than 80 percent of the people around him were below the poverty line. Many of his friends' parents didn't make more than ten dollars per day.[284]

His parents ran a provisional store business and his four siblings all pursued engineering degrees. Two of them even pursued additional MBAs. As he described "(my siblings) were an Asian parent's dream".[285] In comparison, the messy-haired Ritesh was the one who his parents assumed was never going to get anywhere. Their aspiration for him was simple: get a stable job at one of the IT companies. Instead, however, Ritesh derived his energy from being different. As he described to an audience of entrepreneurs in 2015,

(I did things like) writing lines of code, which made me feel that I could do the things that I wanted to instead of things that other people wanted me to do. For example, whenever I would write code, I knew that I could create stars on the screens or men walking on the screen, but if I wanted to run the television I could not because there would be some elder who would run it (instead). I felt it (coding) was a very cool way of being able to do the stuff that you wanted to.... From this (coding) to selling SIM cards (for fun), I did everything that was different as a part of my childhood".[286]

This desire to stand out from the crowd continued even into Ritesh's adolescent years. However, he never had a word for this desire. That all changed one day when his eldest sister returned home from college. She described her experiences as an engineer at an "entrepreneurship fest" to her family, and Ritesh was fascinated. It was the first time he had heard that word. After searching in the Oxford Dictionary, Ritesh discovered that an entrepreneur was "somebody who solves a problem and makes a business along with it." From then on, every time his teachers asked what he wanted to be when he grew up, he would respond "I want to be an entrepreneur!" He laughs as he recounts the story,

It was not an intent; I was just trying to be the smarter kid in the class so the others could ask me "Wow that sounds like a nice word! What does it mean?" I wanted people to think "Wow, you're doing something different!".[287]

After tenth grade, Ritesh's life changed. He scored well in his standardized examinations and—as is custom for the smarter, ambitious, and well-off people in his town—decided to finish high school in the big city. Unlike many of his friends, he chose to finish high school in Kota, a city in northwest India that was three days away by train. The reason? So, he could finally do what he wanted to do without his family interfering.

It was in this family-detached world that Ritesh's dream to become an entrepreneur started to become a reality. Kota was the place where Ritesh started to refine the strategic ambition that would continue to shape his life and the lives of almost a billion others through OYO.

When I came here (Kota), I used to take weekend trains from Kota to Delhi and come to be a part of a lot of these conferences to listen to entrepreneurs. I was very inspired by Rahul Bhatia of InterGlobe and Sid Lal of Eicher (Motors). The reason why I found them innovative is that I feel there are very few Indian consumer products that you can take to any part of the world, and it wouldn't feel out of place. I felt Royal Enfield (Eicher Motors) and InterGlobe were companies like those. When I saw (those) entrepreneurs around me, I felt that I didn't want to surround myself with the other school kids, I wanted to also be an entrepreneur or at least learn from these guys.[288]

After a year of doing nothing except meeting people and reading about start-ups, Ritesh tried his hand at entrepreneurship by creating Oravel in February 2012. The seed of this idea came from a very real problem that Ritesh faced while bumming around:

(At that time) my budget of pocket money was very limited. More often than not the only way to find accommodations was trying to search travel blogs and trying to use locals to connect me to the local landowners. This was when I realized that there is a large opportunity for people like us who travel to various places to have accommodations to stay in and on the other side there is a large supply that is available out there which is not available on any platform but is available in those locales. I felt there was a large problem to be solved both from the consumer side and the demand side which is why we launched Oravel…. It was very similar to the "Airbnb of India" where we basically would connect travelers to hotel and service apartment owners.[289]

By October 2012, Oravel had received funding from investors. While building his company, Ritesh spent most of 2012 and early 2013 bouncing between bed-and-breakfast locations. Every day, he would wake up and stay in a new location. Throughout the day he would work on his company and write emails to bed-and-breakfast owners or service apartment owners whose information he had scraped online. In addition to doing market research, he would ask if they would let him stay for free. Through that period of his life, he spent all his savings living in more than one hundred bed-and-breakfast serviced apartments over a period of six months.[290]

Of course, all his friends thought he was crazy. What little savings he had he was spending hotel-hopping across India to build a failing startup. Eventually, it seemed the naysayers were right: Ritesh went broke and had to sleep on the stairs of the property where he was staying. It would have been logical at this point for Ritesh to pick up the phone, admit failure to his family, and return home. But, fueled by ambition, he refused.

Despite the struggles, Ritesh remarks, "I think that was the most important and the best learning part of my life." It even led to his eureka moment.

While traveling, I realized that the problem of discovery of accommodations was a very small problem. You can find a lot of hotels and guest houses online. The problem was in predictability. If I were to just give you a jigsaw of (my) experiences (staying at these hotels) or what guests would say (it would sound like this): they would book the hotel online then call the hotel owner after landing and the hotel owner wouldn't pick up the phone; they would reach the hotel and there would be no signage; they would go inside and the receptionist would be sleeping topless; their bedroom mattresses would be torn; the sockets would not be working; the ceiling would be leaking; breakfast would have all sorts of issues.

I want to fix predictability. Globally this was never done. Nobody who started a tech brand went out and said we will fix predictability in a space that has many moments of failure.[291]

At nineteen years old, one thing was clear to Ritesh: he didn't just want to build a business, he wanted to create a great impact with a product that people could fall in love with. Unfortunately, Oravel struggled to do this even after receiving seed funding from investors. By May 2013, Ritesh had two choices: giving up by going back to school as his parents desired or persevering to keep the entrepreneurship dream alive.

Unsurprisingly, the ambitious Ritesh chose the latter. His explanation? The regret minimization framework that has guided his entrepreneurial journey.

AMBITION TO CAPTURE THE WORLD

The birth of OYO is inexplicably tied to Ritesh being accepted into the Thiel Fellowship. Founded by technology entrepreneur and early Facebook investor Peter Thiel in 2011, the fellowship is designed for young entrepreneurs under the age of twenty-two. When accepted, these twenty Thiel Fellows are required to skip or stop out of school to receive a $100,000 grant and support from the Thiel Foundation's network to build a world-changing business.

Ritesh applied on a whim on the last day that the application was due in December 2012. He made it to the final round, and after pitching Oravel to the fellowship committee in San Francisco in April 2013, was named a Thiel Fellow. Almost overnight, Ritesh became the poster boy of Indian entrepreneurship.[292]

I was the first Asian resident to be a Thiel Fellow. That was a turning period of my life… There were two things I learned in the fellowship. The first was in the fellowship contract. Its first line said, "As Thiel Fellows we never let university interfere with our education." Education exists everywhere. University is just one of the ways to get it. So, I felt that this is fantastic! You get paid not to go to university! And you still learn! The second thing that I learned was thinking very big…. The first time I was there in the Bay area, I heard this guy who had a company which had twenty customers. He was saying "I want to be the biggest in the world doing this." So, I felt the scale of ambition is just dramatically different…. In India, a lot of venture firms I would meet would always ask me "What is your GC? Not General Council, Global Comparison." So they could tell their Limited Partners and other partners in the US saying that "We are investing in this company (in India) which is an emulator of this company in the US." But there in the Bay Area, I didn't see any of the other entrepreneurs saying, "I am emulating this from Russia." Everybody was building their own new thing, solving a problem.[293]

Ritesh relaunched Oravel as OYO with a new team and returned to India in 2014. Over the years, he had developed a new mindset of ambition: not only did he want to minimize regret, but he also wanted to expand his belief of what was possible. Blending his past experience of hopping from hotel to hotel with his knowledge gained from Oravel and his new global mindset as a Thiel Fellow, Ritesh identified a new problem to solve.

Around the world, every hotel chain was one hundred rooms or larger. But worldwide, 95 percent of the hotels were one hundred rooms or smaller. "Why," Ritesh asked himself, "is no one opening a hotel chain that is one hundred rooms or smaller?"[294] He answered himself with two reasons: "Either one, this is an idea that so many people have tried and failed. Or two, this is something that no one has seen, and I would be the first person seeing it." As an ambitious entrepreneur designed to be an optimist, Ritesh defaulted to the second thought. "The worst thing that could happen was that I would go back to school," he said with a retrospective, knowing smile in 2018 to a crowd of students at their convocation.[295] Of course, the reality of the situation was much closer to his first thought.

Ritesh focused on building OYO in the face of failures that others had experienced. However, he took an entirely new approach. While most entrepreneurs opted to build entirely new hotels, OYO did not want to build or buy new hotels. Instead, they wanted to take advantage of existing hotel infrastructure and make them better. For India, which had an overwhelmingly large middle- and lower-class, OYO's model allowed Ritesh to create a standardized and predictable experience at an extremely low cost.

Ritesh is the first to admit that OYO is not an innovator in creating a business based on standardization and price cuts. Companies like Dominos Pizza had done it long before them. What OYO added was a deep understanding and empathy for guests staying in a hotel. Reminiscing on his one-hundred-day bed-and-breakfast journey, he realized that "a consumer cares about the morning breakfast a lot more than the chandelier in the lobby".[296] This curated list of customer needs and cares is OYO's secret sauce that allows them to ensure that the size of beds, layout of rooms, sheets, Wi-Fi, breakfast, and more are predictable and consistent regardless of which of the 1,300,000 OYO rooms consumers stay in.

As summarized by Harvard Business School,

Unlike other players in the online travel industry, OYO rooms, started in 2013, works as a business aggregator. It takes part of their partner hotel rooms for lease and controls them entirely to provide standardized customer experience to its users. The rooms are branded under the common banner of OYO rooms. They create value by providing budget accommodation at a superior service for the customer. Also, they operate in more than 200 Indian cities thereby extending its services in most parts of the country. Customers can book for the rooms using "OYO rooms" application and through its website.

OYO Rooms captures value by charging customers different sets of prices called 'take up rate.' Their expenses include paying leasing amounts for the partner hotels, and the amount they spend on the leased rooms to standardize the service. OYO rooms pioneered in bringing even zero-to-2-star hotels and guest houses to customers' reach through their site and apps as they standardize their service.[297]

It's clear that Ritesh and OYO are examples of two types of ambition: the ambition to minimize regret and the ambition to capture the world. But this doesn't answer the question that makes OYO a case study as a Unicorn company. How did OYO grow to have sixty-two times the number of locations than Marriott in 7.5 percent of the time? That was caused by a third, and final, type of ambition: trickle-down ambition.

TRICKLE-DOWN AMBITION

Ritesh's success was rapid: by the age of twenty-one he hired fifty employees, by twenty-two he had 500 hotels, and by twenty-four he raised a $1 billion funding round.[298] The more he climbed, the more he began to see a broader horizon of opportunity. However, his true success and the success of OYO is enabling his employees, hotel partners, and investors to also be as ambitious and forward-looking as he is.

During the early days of OYO in 2014, Ritesh was doing everything. When they only had one hotel, he was the customer support representative picking up phones at the call center, the cleaning boy fixing rooms, and the CEO expected to grow the company. As you could imagine, it was an extremely busy time; however, the company was not growing. Bejul Somaia, one of OYO's early investors from

Lightspeed Venture Partners, had an interesting piece of advice for Ritesh. As Ritesh remembers,

He (Bejul) invited me to have lunch with him every month, so I went to have lunch with him. For me, the reason why this lunch used to be great is that Bejul's office is in a fancy five-star hotel, so he used to always treat me to great lunches. For me, meeting him was of course important but more important was a great lunch.

He laughs at the memory and continues:

After the feeding was done, he asked me, "Ritesh, I hear that you've been spending a lot of time on calls and speaking to customers." I said "Of course, absolutely! I love doing that, I could do that all my life!" He said, "That's perfect! So, we now have the head of call centers for OYO. Let's now recruit the CEO." And I of course got the message: it is my job to bring in solid leaders and entrepreneurs who can build the company one level ahead of me so that OYO outgrows one individual and becomes an institution with strong leaders.[299]

After that conversation, Ritesh shifted his focus from driving ambition to trickling-down ambition to his team. He now manages with a perspective of having a microscope in one hand and a telescope in the other. Of course, in the early days, a founder must do everything (the microscope), but as a company grows that same leader must also be able to inspire others to develop their company and look toward long-term visions (the telescope). As Ritesh reflects, "If you look at a broader leadership in the history of our company, not a single

CXO has ever left. Of the eleven CXOs we have, we only keep adding and a majority of them have been there for an 80 percent period or more of the company's existence…. Bringing people who can genuinely be partners is something I have learned as being very, very valuable".[300]

Of course, this is easier said than done. But OYO has two clear examples of inspiring trickle-down ambition in their employees: one at the corporate level and one at the commercial level.

After a few years, the OYO leadership team had built what they called internally "The Cannon." It was a strategic playbook that could take any city or country from nothing and convert a significant part of the hospitality industry into OYO hotels. However, in 2015, ZO Room, a competitor to OYO, launched and began eating into OYO's market share.[301] In an effort to combat the erosion, Ritesh called in his senior leadership team to meet on one Saturday afternoon to strategize and the following Sunday called in his whole one-hundred-person team.

Everyone was angry. And a bunch of leaders said, "Never use a cannon to just take a bird out. Use a cannon to take large animals out." We had built this massive capability, we had a playbook of recruiting, we had a playbook of signing, we had people across the country; all we needed to do was use our capability really well. So, Sunday morning at 10 a.m., the entire office was called. We had close to one hundred people then. And I asked randomly to people, "How many properties can we sign in the next one month?" Someone said "Thirty-five." That was the maximum. Somebody said "Twenty-six."

Someone else said "Thirty-one" and so on. I said, "No. We're going to add one hundred properties next month." That was a five-time jump and people thought to themselves, "This guy has gone bonkers. He's just another entrepreneur losing his mind".[302]

As you may already have guessed, Ritesh was not losing his mind. In fact, when he presented "The Cannon" to his employees, they were in awe. It was a structure that split cities up into clusters and used standardized tricks to complete signing, auditing, branding, and launching with ownership decided by cluster.

The project was nicknamed the MI100, or the Mission Impossible 100, an homage to one of Ritesh's favorite movies. The OYO team was energized by the vision, ambition, and humor.

Thirty days later, the team had a follow-up meeting. In that meeting, they revealed that just in Delhi alone, OYO had signed 130 properties. MI100 was a massive success and was expanded across the country. By the end of the year, OYO had signed 4,500 hotels and successfully trickled down the ambition of the senior leadership team. And ZO Room? By 2016, OYO acquired them.

It was one of the most amazing things our company has done.[303]

At the commercial level, OYO has innovated on the model of housekeeping pay, which in turn has inspired more trickle-down ambition. In traditional hospitality businesses, housekeepers are paid a salary throughout the year. Thus, the top 20 percent of housekeepers get paid the same as the bottom 20 percent. At OYO, every employee has a mobile app, and they get paid based on the number of rooms that they clean. This has led to three surprising benefits.[304]

First, the mobile app removes the need to have individual floor managers to determine which room needs to be cleaned. Because housekeepers are paid by the number of rooms cleaned, they are inspired to seek out this information themselves and act on it before their coworkers. The second benefit is that it has inspired housekeepers to clean rooms better because of in-app bonuses based on performance. After a room is cleaned, guests can rate the quality of cleaning, and higher ratings are tied to bonus compensation. Third, this mobile-app-model has given housekeepers a sense of ownership to innovate on faster cleaning techniques. What new chemicals could they use? What new processes exist? What tools can they buy to clean a room faster? All these questions are not thrust top-down, but instead surfaced bottom-up from an employee's self-developing ambition. In this sense, the term "OYOpreneurs" truly is an homage to the entrepreneurial mindset that Ritesh hopes all OYO employees will naturally adopt.

Even today, that ambition continues; as Ritesh remarked at the end of his lecture *How to Start a Startup*, "We are 0.1 percent of what we will become".[305]

STRIVING FOR EXCELLENCE

Ritesh's "overnight success" is a five- to ten-year story. But what *is* success for India's youngest billionaire?

When I am forty years old or fifty years old, what will make me happy? Will I be happy about building something where you land in any part of the world, and you walk out of the airport and point to that and say I built this company? Or will I be happy if I was the person who made some money early in my life? The answer is straight forward. I am much happier being the former. Being someone who did something impactful with my life rather than the person who had more money for myself. That is the strive for excellence that I request for everyone to have.[306]

Excellence for Ritesh and OYO lies in strategic ambition: minimizing regret, expanding world views, and trickling down inspiration. This mentality is the key to unlocking the OYO Unicorn. It is the way to understand the boy who seven years ago was a nobody, but today is having dinner with presidents.

So now to the burning question: what does OYO stand for? On Your Own: a fitting homage for a founder whose strategic ambitions forced him to create opportunities on his own terms.

Chapter Summary

Lesson 1. One of Donald Trump's favorite Indian entrepreneurs is Ritesh Agarwal, a billionaire who dropped out of college. Ritesh discovered entrepreneurship after his sister taught him the term when she returned home from college. He was inspired by Rahul Bhatia of InterGlobe and Sid Lal of Eicher Motors because they sought to solve problems globally by creating Indian consumer products. After living in bed-and-breakfasts for six months as a nineteen-year-old, Ritesh realized the problem he wanted to solve: predictability in housing. This was the beginning of OYO (which, notably, was not his first startup; his first startup was a failure).

Lesson 2. Ritesh has a quote that has guided his life: "Whenever I have two opportunities, risking it versus regretting it, I will always invariably choose risking it because I will never want to regret that I did not pursue something that I really want to do." This regret minimization framework is similar to that of Jeff Bezos and led Ritesh to apply (and be accepted) as the first Asian resident to be a Thiel Fellow. It forced Ritesh to find education everywhere and think of his businesses as global-by-default. As an individual, Ritesh was immensely successful in trickling down this ambition to the rest of his team as well.

Lesson 3. The key innovation in OYO was seeing what no one else bothered touching. Around the world, every hotel chain was one hundred rooms or larger, but 95 percent of the hotels in the world were one hundred rooms or smaller. OYO's innovation was to design a business focused on the small- and medium-sized hotel industry. The strategy involved using existing hotel infrastructure, improving the hotels, and unifying these assets under one consistent brand. They cut the frills and focused on what customers care about. As Ritesh reminisced, "A consumer cares about the morning breakfast a lot more than the chandelier in the lobby."

CHAPTER 9:

PARTNERSHIP DECACORN

———

Starting a centralized Unicorn business in Southeast Asia is both heaven and hell.

Let's start with the fire.

As a startup founder, dominating the whole of Southeast Asia is nearly impossible because of its immense diversity and difference of consumers. The region referred to as "Southeast Asia" is composed of eleven different countries (Brunei, Myanmar, Cambodia, Timor-Leste, Indonesia, Laos, Malaysia, the Philippines, Singapore, Thailand, and Vietnam) with citizens who speak more than nine different languages (Lao, Thai, Burmese, Khmer, Vietnamese, Tagalog, Malay, Indonesian and also a peppering of Chinese dialects) and practice over seven of the world's major religions (Hinduism, Buddhism, Sikhism, Jainism, Christianity, Islam, Judaism, and Zoroastrianism).

Moreover, every country has its own regulatory structures, abides by its own laws, and uses its own currency with unique exchange rates. Comparing these countries to one another economically through a measure of GDP exacerbates this difference: while Indonesia has a GDP of $1.042 trillion (with a T), Timor-Leste and Cambodia have GDPs of $2.581 billion and $24.54 billion respectively (with a B). These numbers certainly aren't helped by the fact that only 27 percent of those living in Southeast Asia have a bank account.[307]

But, with every fire comes a bit of warmth.

Southeast Asia's saving grace is its sheer size and continuous development. Over 670 million people live in Southeast Asia (more than the US and UK combined) and account for 8.58 percent of the world's population. Numerically, Indonesia is the fourth most populous country in the world after China, India, and the United States with 270 million people spread out across more than 17,000 islands.[308]

In addition to population numbers today, Southeast Asia is seeing massive growth and potential for the future. The average age of a Southeast Asian citizen is 30.1 years old; the region is growing at almost 6 percent a year (compared to the US' modest 3 percent per year) as reported by the World Bank, and according to Japanese consulting company Mitsui & Co., all five major cities in Southeast Asia (not including Singapore) are expected to become megacities with populations of over ten million in the near future.

Though fragmented socially, politically, and economically, Southeast Asia is a region ripe for growth to entrepreneurs looking for a challenge.

Perhaps the most successful to date are Anthony Tan and Hooi Ling Tan, two Harvard Business School classmates turned co-founders. In 2012, they created Grab, a transportation company headquartered in Singapore which started as an Uber copycat but now has seen immense success as one of two Superapps in Southeast Asia (the other, Gojek, was founded by Nadiem Makarim, another Harvard Business School classmate).

In the last nine years, Grab has raised over $11 billion from investors like Softbank, Microsoft, Booking.com, Toyota, and Didi Chuxing.[309] In short, investors have valued Grab's existence at over $3 million a day. In a move that made headlines, Grab acquired Uber's Southeast Asia operations in 2018 in exchange for Uber owning 27 percent of Grab and Dara Khosrowshahi (Uber's CEO) joined their board.[310] Despite the $9.5 million in fines that Grab had to pay after the Uber merger, in 2019 alone Grab still had more than $2 billion in revenue.[311]

Studying the story of Hooi Ling Tan, Grab's female co-founder, is a key to understanding how to use partnership to unlock a Southeast Asian Decacorn (a company ten times more valuable than a Unicorn). Despite battles with Uber, anti-trust lawsuits, and operating in over 350 cities, three types of partnership have prevailed to push Grab to success: internal partnership between co-founders, customer partnerships with "Grabbers," and strategic partnerships with governments and competitors.

INTERNAL PARTNERSHIPS: UNLIKELY CO-FOUNDERS

Hooi Ling Tan grew up as the youngest and only daughter in a family of four. As a teenager in Malaysia in the 1990s, she was a self-described "gadget freak" who was "always interested in figuring out how things worked".[312] Perhaps, she picked up this curiosity for tinkering from her father who was a civil engineer. "I always liked logic, physics, and math and enjoyed seeing my father tear apart stuff to try and fix it".[313] Her mother was a stockbroker remisier (agent), and since both of her parents worked, Hooi Ling settled in to a life in the middle class.

To be honest it was what you'd expect any other family to go through. Public schooling in Malaysia, where I learned everything in Bahasa (a dialect of Malay, the official language of Malaysia). I only really picked up English very well when I went to undergrad in England.[314]

They lived in a semi-detached house in Petaling Jaya about twenty minutes away from Kuala Lumpur. In her free-time, Hooi Ling would play sports like badminton or instruments like the piano or violin. Growing up, she and her brother "used to fight a lot but I love him like to- I don't want to use the word death, but that's how much I love him. A lot. I respect him a lot".[315]

After high school, Hooi Ling convinced her parents to let her study mechanical engineering at the University of Bath in Britain, an homage to her father's tinkering. Despite her parents' reluctance, she traveled 10,000 kilometers for schooling, and eventually, even took a year off to work at Eli Lilly, the pharmaceutical company, at one of their manufacturing plants in Basingstoke, England.[316]

I was helping them to figure out how to use their equipment more efficiently, health safety standards, all those things. It was a really good learning opportunity.... That's when I said: "Hey, I need to step back." Mechanical engineering, despite what I initially thought and loved, was not going to be the future I wanted to spend all my time on. What I wanted to do was really understand how businesses make decisions.[317]

She finished her engineering degree and returned just twenty minutes away from her childhood home to work at McKinsey & Company in Kuala Lumpur. After long twelve-hour days, Hooi Ling would have to find some way to safely get herself back home. At that time, Kuala Lumpur was known as one of the worst cities to take a taxi in terms of safety and reliability. This is where the inspiration for Grab came from.

If you were to Google "world's worst taxi" fifteen years ago, the top hit for the first page or two would have been Kuala Lumpur, which is Malaysia's city capital. That's the environment we grew up in. Even worse, the moment I became an adult, I was working late at McKinsey, so there was no real alternative. I couldn't drive myself home because I would fall asleep in the car; it was late nights. My mom and I developed

a manual GPS tracking system. Back then, during the Nokia
good old phone days, (there were) no smartphones and no
GPS tracking. I would literally text her the car number plates,
the name of the driver, and the license of the taxi I got into. I
would also text her whenever I hit any of the major milestones
or landmarks that we would pre-agree on so that she would
know if I was fifteen minutes away, seven minutes away, or
just around the corner. Every single night she would sleep on
our couch waiting for me.[318]

However, it wasn't until four years later, when Hooi Ling
met Anthony Tan, her business partner, that this seed of
experiential inspiration would begin to grow into a Decacorn.

While Hooi Ling was taking late night taxi rides to and from
work, Anthony Tan was working at Tan Chong Motor Group,
the family business started by his grandfather. Tan Chong
Motors, an almost $1 billion company, operates in Malaysia
and Singapore and was the family business that Anthony
was supposed to inherit and run with his Harvard Business School diploma in hand. He dabbled a bit in the family
business during his early twenties after he graduated from
the University of Chicago (where he studied Economics and
Public Policy). As the son of the CEO, Anthony developed
an understanding of the business from the ground up. He
started in the factory then quickly became the head of supply
chain and marketing at Tan Chong Group, where he drove
logistics and created brand affinity for the automotive brands
under the group.[319]

I had to go through and do my own thing. I worked in a factory
and would get on a bus at 4:30 in the morning with our own

teammates to assemble cars. I think those experiences humbled me and taught me a lot in life's lessons.[320]

Luckily, by the time Hooi Ling met Anthony at Harvard Business School, he had shed the stereotypical "rich kid" aura and developed the empathy to create businesses with a double bottom line.

Hooi Ling and Anthony met often as HBS classmates during Asian community food gatherings. Unlike prior years, the 2011 HBS class had five Malaysians, a departure from the usual two or three per year. At first, Hooi Ling was apprehensive to meet Anthony, thinking that "He's probably very different from us because he comes from a rich family...when I meet him, I'll meet him, but I have no real intent of going to meet him." However, by the end of the first year, she found him to be "very atypical.... He's actually way more hard-working than I was, super humble and just a nice person to be with".[321]

By their second year, they were in two courses together: Business at the Base of the Pyramid (about how business can significantly improve the quality of life for people in developing countries) and Launching Technology Ventures. The pair quickly became friends.[322] As Anthony recalls,

She didn't do the homework. I did the homework and she copied my homework.[323]

They both laugh as they recall their time at HBS. Through classes and discussions, Hooi Ling and Anthony realized that their world views were more similar than different. By the end of that year, they had enrolled their idea, MyTeksi, in the fifteenth annual $150,000 Harvard Business Plan Contest. After competing with sixty-three other teams, they placed second in the Social Venture Track, eventually winning $10,000 in cash and $10,000 of in-kind services like advisors.[324]

Though unlikely co-founders from entirely different backgrounds, Hooi Ling and Anthony worked well together. After business school, Anthony took the risk of entrepreneurship rather than going into his family business to build out MyTeksi. Using some of his mother's money as seed funding, he built a team in Kuala Lumpur and began to develop the software for what is now known as Grab.[325] In the meantime, Hooi Ling returned to McKinsey for her one year of required post-business school employment. She then spent two more years working at Salesforce to "figure out how to learn from technology companies globally and bring that back to Southeast Asia." Despite this, even while at Salesforce, Hooi Ling was spending her free time to helping Grab grow through unpaid work.[326]

Because I (Hooi Ling) was doing this in my spare time, I had to take holidays to come back to Southeast Asia to spend time with the team. Once I took a two-week holiday, the moment I landed I started a five-country sprint of work. I told my bosses at Salesforce, and they found all of it really funny and they understood my passion. They gave me time for it as well.[327]

Eventually, after two years at Salesforce, Hooi Ling uprooted herself to work on Grab full time as the Chief Operating Officer. Today, their offices have over forty-five nationalities working at the company, operate in eight countries, and have R&D centers in the United States (Seattle), India (Bangalore), and China (Beijing).

I think one of the surprises I shared earlier was our ability to get to where we are today. It's not because of what Anthony or I have done or what we can do, but more because of the great fellow Grabbers (the drivers and customers who use Grab) and individuals we've been able to attract along this journey. It's been extremely surprising and heartening to know that so many other Southeast Asians actually care about the same problems that we do and actually want to invest a lot of blood, sweat, and tears into solving it…. We are continuously going to learn and iterate and grow together to make Grab a company that will shape Southeast Asia's future.[328]

Part of what allowed Grab to nab its $10 billion valuation was the unique perspective that Hooi Ling has (as a middle-class female from Southeast Asian traveling to and from work late at night) combined with Anthony (the grandson of a tycoon with resources as one of the wealthiest families of Malaysia). The key to unlocking the Grab Unicorn is in partnership: especially internally within the operating team itself.

CUSTOMER PARTNERSHIP: PARTNER-FIRST MENTALITY

Internal partnership, however, does not guarantee success. Even with both Hooi Ling and Anthony on the ground working on Grab, they had to compete with the monstrous elephant in the room: Uber. As Anthony reflected in 2014,

Uber's emergence within the region has opened the doors for us to strive for the better. The introduction of the GrabTaxi app was the initial phase of disruption for the taxi industry.

Taxi drivers have been stuck in the rut for the longest time, but Uber's rise has helped us to push taxi drivers to take them to the next level. We've opened their eyes and ears for them to improve themselves and their service to remain relevant.

We never rest on our laurels and say we've done enough. That is not something GrabTaxi will ever do. My team and I are constantly challenging ourselves to be able to remain the largest and most dominant player in this region.[329]

While helpful, Grab still had to compete with the company that had billions in funding to win the regional market. Their focus? Hyper-localization and an intense desire to listen to their "Grabbers," or the drivers and customers who use Grab. There were three areas of these hyper-localized customer partnerships, which helped Grab beat Uber to become the dominant player in the region: acquiring their first Grabbers, durian fruits, and introducing cashless payments.

Today, Grab offers services such as GrabCar, GrabCar+, GrabBike, GrabFamily, JustGrab, and GrabHitch to cater to more diverse needs of clients.[330] But when they first launched, they had only one service: GrabTaxi. To acquire their first customers, Anthony literally knocked on the doors of random taxi drivers sitting in their cars.

It was tough. Really tough. We would set up a plastic table that probably costs two US dollars right by the monsoon drains beside gas stations because taxis would come by gas stations. We would say "Hey Uncle! Give us a shot! We will give you some Nasi Lemak!" which is a breakfast rice and a little drink that cost twenty cents. Then if they didn't have a smartphone, we would subsidize phones for them. Then in Singapore, Jakarta, or wherever, literally where we knew nobody, we would knock on windows while they were lining up at an airport or buying gas at a station to convince them one by one (to use Grab).[331]

The mentality that Anthony, Hooi Ling, and the team embraced was one of treating their drivers as partners and employees rather than simply products or cogs in the machine. The face-to-face interactions with the Grab team and customized smartphones were evidence of Grab's partnership-first mentality. They treated their drivers as part of a broader family with the aim of uplifting their livelihoods. Hooi Ling even went one step further:

I remember when we first started the company, I had to go and do training sessions with our first few batches of drivers to help teach them how to use a smartphone. They had never seen one before. They had never touched one before. They had no idea how to turn on Wi-Fi or what GPS was. Trust me, the kind of problem-solving sessions we had back then were just (answering the question) "How do we help teach our drivers to use these basic technologies that are already available?" Those problems still exist.[332]

While Uber was selling a refined product from a headquarters in the United States almost 13,000 kilometers away from Malaysia, Grab thrived by building genuine partnerships designed to build drivers' skills. Free breakfast, drinks, phones, and training were the fundamental building blocks of Grab's success.

This on-the-ground campaigning also led to a home-court advantage that even Uber couldn't have predicted. Following their successful playbook, whenever Uber launched in a new location, they would host an "Uber Ice Cream" campaign. The one-day stunt allowed Uber users to request ice cream delivery to their location through their mobile app. At its peak, the response was huge with over 300,000 ice creams delivered to its users in 252 cities around the world.[333] Unfortunately, in Malaysia the campaign was not nearly as successful.

Uber had a great campaign: on-demand Uber ice cream. We (Grab) didn't think that would fly because it's hot in the region, so it melts and getting slushy ice cream ain't fun (Instead) we asked, "What do Singaporeans, Malaysians, Thai love?" The king of fruits: the durian. In over thirty days we sold twenty-five tons of durian, making us the biggest durian seller in Singapore.[334]

The innovative campaign was a huge risk that paid off. Durian is known as the "smelliest fruit in the world," and in many parts of Southeast Asia, it is banned from hotels and public transport.[335] Despite this, it is an extremely popular fruit and begot a surge in Grab usage instead of Uber. In large part, this campaign was fueled by an intense knowledge of and partnership with local farmers, drivers, and culture to create a uniquely localized campaign. After three years of these annual campaigns, Grab eventually acquired Uber's Southeast Asian unit in 2018: a sweet win for a smelly fruit.

In addition to Grabber relations and durian, Grab has also thrived due to their intentional partnerships to integrate cashless payments into a culture that is largely still cash based. This is a challenge that has been solved by Grab primarily through deep trust with customers, and of course, hyper-localization. As Hooi Ling described at the 2016 RISE conference,

Southeast Asia is a cash-based economy. Ninety-five percent of individuals prefer cash and only 5 percent use credit cards. And even if they use it, they don't want to put it in some app.… When Grab first started, we started monetizing on a cash basis. We started taking cash from our drivers and getting them to transact by creating a credit wallet so that they could have credits to continue accepting jobs.… Southeast Asia is a cash-based economy, but that's not going to be the case going forward. We can already see that change. Grab has now been in the market for four years.… Ultimately, we have been able to get the trust of our consumers because they understand we're in it for the long run.[336]

While counterintuitive, Grab had a deep understanding and relationship with customers which beat out competitors in the market. Despite having a smaller team, less funding, and an underdeveloped product, Grab is a perfect case study for understanding the value of partnership with treating customers with a partner-first mentality. Today, these investments have not only paid off for grab, but also for Southeast Asia as a whole. Just in 2018, Grab contributed $5.8 billion in direct impact to the Southeast Asian countries they serve by enabling nine million micro-entrepreneurs and enabling one in seventy Southeast Asians to earn an additional income stream.[337]

Grab's double-bottom line is achieved through a partnership mentality of deeply understanding customers and is the second component of unlocking the Grab Partnership Decacorn.

STRATEGIC PARTNERSHIPS: PARTNER, BUILD, BUY IN THAT ORDER

From Day One, Grab has been in the business of finding the smartest people then enabling them to do the best work possible. Hooi Ling and Anthony both adopt a Socratic mindset: they know that they don't know everything, and rather than pretending to be the smartest, they welcome partnering with governments and traditional competitors as a means to growth.

For us (Grab), we look for the best global partners. We partner with companies like Microsoft or Booking.com for hotel bookings. We also partner with the best local banks in each country, for example Maybank, UOB, or KBank. The reason for this is that we are trying to understand what our specific customer needs and who has the best solution for it. If they exist in the world somewhere around us and we believe that we can work together to achieve that long-term vision, we will happily shake hands, sign a piece of paper, and work together in the long term. When that happened with Softbank and Toyota, I think it was fantastic.[338]

The idea of partnering to grow in Southeast Asia is no surprise: eleven different countries beget eleven different legal systems, eleven different economies, and eleven different norms to operate around. Logistically, one of the best ways to grow quickly and nimbly with one centralized product is through partnership with knowledgeable local players. What is so striking, however, is the success that Grab has seen in partnership. While other companies look to the framework of "Build, Buy, or Partner," Grab flips this conception on its head. "At Grab we go through the typical Build, Buy, or Partner thinking. Except our sequence of how we think about it is usually different. We say: 'Partner or not? If not Partner, build or not? If not build, should we acquire'"?[339] Unlike typical organizations, this mentality permeates Grab and is the mindset that all employees take.

Though unconventional, this approach has led to immense success.

What has been great is that our partners, both public and private, have seen from the consistency of our actions and our intent that we actually have shared visions, aspirations, and intentions. What we want to do is help make things better for the citizens of Southeast Asia. We started with transportation and mobility, but there is so much more right now. Whether it's financial inclusion, whether it's empowering micro-entrepreneurs and small entrepreneurs, or whether it's making healthcare and education better—there is so much more that we can do, and they have seen us take action on it.... Therefore, they trust us much more than they initially did.[340]

In the numbers, this is also strikingly clear. In less than a year, Grab was able to acquire six licenses from six different governments to begin rolling out their mobile wallet features to customers. Most other companies and competitors take multiple years to get any one of these licenses. Grab thrived in having preexisting relationships with governments and local banks to strategically partner for growth. The secret was watering the spouts of these relationships through good will and consistent action even before asking for anything from their partners.[341]

The final area where Grab thrives in their strategic partnership is through their composition of the board of directors. With a board comprised of members like Toyota, Softbank, Didi, and Uber, Hooi Ling and Anthony are surrounded by advisors and partners from nearly every relevant industry to ride-sharing or finance. "That end-to-end view," Hooi Ling describes, "of being able to shape the future not just from a technology and consumer behavior standpoint but also from the hardware is going to be super critical in the longer game…. There is so much to do, and we don't want to do it all alone".[342] This mentality of making 1+1 = 3 is a core, differentiating factor that Grab uniquely had to adopt in order to grow and unify the untapped and fragmented Southeast Asian market.

Today, Grab's ethos of partnership is fundamental to the company's new strategy: rather than simply building a ride-sharing business, Grab wants to become the Super-app of Southeast Asia. The goal? To unify everything that a typical consumer does in one day on a single pane of glass all powered from the familiar green user interface. As this

Decacorn continues to grow into a Centicorn and beyond, it is clear that the key to their success has been, and will continue to be, their three major pillars of partnership: internal, customer, and strategic.

Chapter Summary

Lesson 1. With more than twenty thousand islands, Southeast Asia is one of the most fragmented and diverse regions in the world. Building a unified, centralized company is extremely difficult. Nonetheless, through partnership with a variety of entities, Anthony Tan and Hooi Ling Tan of Grab were able to defy the odds and create the largest ride-sharing companies and Superapps in the region. The highlight of this ride was Grab's acquisition of Uber's Southeast Asia operations. Though the two co-founders come from entirely different worlds (Anthony is the son of multi-millionaires and Hooi Ling was a child of the middle class), they met at Harvard and bonded over their desire to create businesses in the developing world.

Lesson 2. One of the biggest competitors that Grab had to fend off in the early days was Uber: the $90 billion elephant in the room. Even though Uber was significantly larger, Grab competed through hyper-localization: they acquired drivers through door-to-door campaigns (literally knocking on doors), localized marketing campaigns (using durian fruits), and innovations that Uber hadn't yet implemented (like cashless payments). While Uber was 13,000 kilometers away, Grab thrived by being able to build genuine partnerships on the ground and adapt in real time.

Lesson 3. Partnership has been the "secret sauce" of Grab. Operating in eleven different countries has forced their team to be nimble and grow through finding localized players who have knowledge. Rather than adopting the traditional "Build, Buy, Partner" model, Grab adopts a "Partner, Build, Buy" model (in that order). They always strive to partner with industry players before building their own solution. This 1+1=3 mentality has led to quick roll-out and government approvals for what would normally be controversial features.

CHAPTER 10:

CONTENT-MARKET FIT

———

Growing up as a Ghanaian born in America, I was exposed to music from West Africa on a daily basis. My mother and father would play the artists and songs that turned Seattle's gray skies into the lazy heat of Ghana's sun. No song reminds me of the jollof rice, peanut soup, and fufu I ate as a child more than Yaa Amponsah. Recorded in 1928, Yaa Amponsah is instantly recognizable as one of the most popular highlife songs. In the original recordings, guitar pricks resonate off palm wine, lyrical Twi voices soar above the beats of kpanlogo drums, and an airy breath reminiscent of a tropical summer's breeze whisper into my ears. Its rhythms are to West Africans what twelve-bar jazz and blues are to African Americans.[343]

Despite Yaa Amponsah's significance, whenever I traveled to my parents' home in Ghana, I would rarely hear it.[344] Instead, I heard the same music that I listened to in the United States. Rather than listening to Koo Nimo or E.T. Mensah, Ghanaian peers my age listened to Kesha and Eminem. Why?

This phenomenon doesn't just exist in Ghana.

All over the world, English music from English-speaking artists dominates the music or language of a listener's home country. Nielsen in 2018 confirmed this with an analysis of the Top 200 most-streamed songs around the world across all major streaming services (YouTube, Spotify, Apple Music, and Amazon Music). They discovered that English language music made up 67 percent of the top 200, followed by Spanish at a distant 18 percent, and Hindi at 6 percent.[345] That same analysis also discovered that the top five countries of origin for artists were the US, the UK, India, Puerto Rico, and Colombia in that order.[346]

Why is it that even though only 20 percent of the world speaks English, almost 70 percent of the world's most popular streamed music is in English?

One region has slowly begun to change this statistic: Korea. More specifically, K-Pop (Korean Pop Music). The export of K-Pop had ballooned South Korea's music industry to an impressive and growing $5 billion industry in 2017.[347] In 2018, the South Korean music market experienced a 17.9 percent revenue growth to become a power player as the sixth largest music market worldwide.[348]

Most consumers' first interaction with K-Pop was through Park Jae-sang, also known as PSY. In 2012, Park put South Korea on the map by releasing the viral song "Gangnam Style." For more than five years, it held the record for most watched YouTube video of all time at more than 3.9 billion views as of January 2020.[349] The hit featured electronic beats and an infectiously simple dance with loose hands, sturdy hips, and horse-like hops.

K-Pop, however, is much older than PSY. Historians almost unanimously seem to agree that it was born on April 11, 1992.

In 1992, just after South Korea's 1987 reformation of its government, national South Korean TV networks penetrated 99 percent of South Korean homes and the network's weekend talent shows were the biggest source of entertainment and cultural impact.[350] At one of these talent shows on April 11, 1992, Seo Taiji and Boys performed "Nan Arayo (I Know)".[351] Dancing on stage in baggy baseball button ups and overalls, the Boys performed one of the first ever Korean American pop fusions. While they lost the talent show, "I Know" went on to top South Korea's singles charts for a record-smashing seventeen weeks, which would stand for more than fifteen years as the longest No. 1 streak in the country's history.[352]

In a bang, K-Pop was let out of the bottle.

By the end of the decade, the three powerhouse music studios of K-Pop were born and the global ecosystem for a billion-dollar music business was cultured. The three studios, SM Entertainment (often referred to as SM Town) in 1995, JYP Entertainment in 1997, and YG Entertainment in 1998, began to deliberately cultivate what would become known as K-Pop idol groups with a focus on not just creating great music, but developing dances, celebrity personalities, and superfans.[353]

Soon these Korean pop idols started to become famous outside of Korea too. In 2003, singer BoA and boy band TVXQ became the first K-Pop idols to break into the Japanese market, and with support from the South Korean government who had an eye on economic potential, the K-Pop wave started to spread farther to an even more global audience. Today, barely thirty years after a niche segment on a Saturday evening talent show, K-Pop has international influence.[354] In 2019, girl band Blackpink was the first K-Pop band to headline Coachella, and in 2020, the Korea foundation estimated that there are more than ninety-nine million K-Pop fans globally.[355]

Perhaps the most successful K-Pop idol group is the seven-member boy band Bangtan Boys, or BTS for short.

As a brand, BTS is a national treasure bringing $3.6 billion to the South Korean economy in 2018 (including $1.2 billion in exports of BTS-related merchandise) and 800,000 visitors to South Korea annually (about 7 percent of the country's annual tourists).[356] Many analysts expect this figure to increase to $37 billion over the next decade.[357] In just 2020 alone, the group broke seven music-related Guinness World Records including most viewed YouTube video (and music video) in twenty-four hours, most weeks at #1 on Billboard Social 50 chart (a ranking of the most-engaged-with musician accounts on social media), and most viewers for a live-streamed music concert.[358] It's no surprise that as of January 2021, BTS had been nominated for over 500 national and international music awards and won more than 280 of them.

Still not convinced of their significance? Well, in 2019 BTS became the first band since the Beatles to have three Billboard No. 1 albums in one year.[359] If you haven't heard of them yet, you undoubtably will soon, even after they're gone.

So how did this group of seven boys grow to be a significant player in the global music industry to win awards and even be invited to speak at the United Nations?

In large part, the success of BTS lies in the vision and abilities of Bang Si-Hyuk, the mastermind behind the boy band and the founder of Big Hit Entertainment. Also knows as Hitman and Bang PD, Bang's journey to bring BTS to stardom started in middle school as a dream. Today, as a member of the Academy for the Grammys, Bang has changed the way that the world sees K-Pop and Korean artists. And in the process, he not only created a Unicorn business (his company Big Hit Entertainment is valued at over $7 billion), but also became a billionaire himself with an estimated net worth of $1.4 billion.[360]

Studying the story of Bang is the key to unlocking the BTS Unicorn and the extremely important concept of content-market fit, which BTS has perfected to crush the charts with every release despite competing in an English-dominated global music market. Their content reflects the lives of the artists, their market taps into the "BTS army," and their fit exploits their content and market to grow exponentially. As Bang describes,

BTS, a group that was born from a small label in East Asia has turned into a global sensation. People all over the world went wild over a music video where Koreans danced and sang in Korean. They voluntarily translated, analyzed, and shared BTS' songs, conversations, and messages and made BTS the Beatles of the YouTube era. The heroes of the periphery.[361]

THE CONTENT (& ITS CREATORS)

Bang's introduction to the music industry started when he was in middle school through a chance encounter.

I'm a typical Billboard kid. It began from when I saw a flower boy band in a very low-quality video through my friend by chance when I was a middle school student.[362]

The video he watched was of Duran Duran, the 1978 English pop band with twenty-one Billboard 100 songs, two Grammy awards, and more than 100 million albums sold. They looked cool, handsome, and Bang liked their music even if he couldn't understand all the words they said. Even today, you can tell that he still lives in boyish glee, thinking about the music group.

He chuckles as he reflects on this formative memory: "Now that I think about it, seeing that I was fixated on a flower boy band from the start, is it destiny?"[363]

Bang took it one step further by creating music as well, "I did a band in middle school," he says with a beaming smile. "The first song I wrote in my life was a metal song I wrote in middle school…. In fact, my cassette tapes were circulated in a nearby girls' school".[364]

Growing up with a love of international music, it was difficult for Bang (a child of the 1970s) to purchase the English band's actual albums. It was even harder to watch videos of them performing. For Bang, consuming music required listening to or viewing the copy, of a copy, of a copy of the original. In

South Korea between 1970 and 1980, this was a phenomenon around South Korea and globally.

Despite his obsession with music, Bang still remained a strong student in school and performed well enough to be accepted to Seoul National University. With a 0.5 percent acceptance rate in 2018 according to national news sources, SNU is billed as the Harvard of South Korea. He graduated near the top of his class with the second-highest GPA from the aesthetics department where he focused his studies.[365]

In 1995, toward the end of his college career, Bang competed in the Yoo JaeHa Song Festival, a rite of passage for any young composer. His submitted work won a bronze statue at the competition.[366] This gave him the legitimacy to break into the industry. By graduation he received an offer from Park Jin-young (a legendary producer and founder of JYP entertainment, one of the big three South Korean entertainment studios) to compose K-Pop hits as a founding team member.[367] The duo with Park as lyricist and Bang as composer, arranger, and producer was phenomenally successful. His success with artists like g.o.d., rain, teen top, 2AM, and Wondergirls earned him the nickname "Hitman Bang".[368]

Working at JYP, Bang learned the process for making a K-Pop star, which in essence was shared at each of the three South Korean entertainment companies. The process mostly focused around three steps: finding talent (typically youth between thirteen and fifteen years old), training these prospects, and launching the most promising trainees in as a group or solo act.[369] While successful, Bang always felt conflicted over two issues: first, were these manufactured groups truly "musicians" and second, didn't the trainee system restrict individuality too much?

As JYP began to grow and expand to US operations, Bang was not satisfied as just a composer. In 2005 he struck out on his own to create Big Hit Entertainment where he began to re-think South Korean talent and entertainment agencies from the ground up.

To me, in the words of Nokia CEO, Big Hit Entertainment is the platform on which my life as a musician is based. It is a place to express my musical desires and to communicate with the public. From where everything starts, I have to keep it. It's something I won't stop doing.[370]

Bang's focus with the firm was to find talented trainees who loved music and bear responsibility for what they do. Unlike other competitors, he hyper-focused on selecting self-motivated talent that fit into the role of the group as a whole.

With this relentless focus and Bang's resumé behind him, Big Hit started to get traction. Annually, Big Hit now gets more than twenty thousand applicants every year to join their K-Pop idol training program with thirty to forty short-listed annually. Each idol is trained holistically in dancing, singing, acting, and photography for three years at a cost of over $100,000 per year. Ultimately, from every dozen trainees, only one is launched to become a K-Pop idol. What set Big Hit apart, however, was Bang's focus on the individual: in addition to typical training, he also offered mental health training, nutrition training, and even mentorship for all his idols.[371]

Unfortunately, it was not all smooth sailing. Within five years, Big Hit was on the brink of bankruptcy. Despite their initial formulations of focusing on idols and idol training, something was not working.

In a last-minute effort to save the business, Bang called the employees together for an intense, internal workshop to reflect retrospectively and create a formula for success. In this search, they asked three pivotal questions, laying the foundation for BTS' success in developing a content-market fit strategy.

1. *What is an idol?*
2. *What is the business we (Big Hit Entertainment) are in?*
3. *Who are the fans and what are their characteristics?*[372]

This pivotal workshop developed the two key insights that still drive BTS to this day. First, most entertainment companies and artists were not using technology effectively to pull people together. Instead, technology and technology platforms like Facebook and Twitter were dividing people and making them increasingly isolated. Second, while idols were important, the fans were the true foundation of any entertainment business. Rather than having an idol-first mentality, Bang's focus shifted to filling a need in what fan's identified as an untapped market.

Immediately, Big Hit began restructuring their whole idol training program and refining the content they produced to better appeal to the insights they had garnered about technology as a connector and interacting with fans. Existing trainees who didn't fit the new model were removed from the program and Bang began building a new idol group from the ground-up: BTS.

At the time that I started my company, physical album sales were abruptly going down and digital sales were not coming up to compensate. But K-Pop idol groups had an advantage in that they had many opportunities to diversify revenue streams and their fans were extremely passionate, allowing concerts to compensate for dropped album sales….

I had considered putting together a hip-hop crew, not an idol group, but when I considered the business context, I thought a K-Pop idol model made more sense. Because many trainees wanted to pursue hip-hop and didn't want to be in an idol band, they left. At that time RM, Suga, and J-hope stayed back, and they remain BTS's musical pillars. From there, through audition, we discovered and added members that had more of an idol-like quality to the group.[373]

By the end of 2013, after the rebrand and the switch, Bang had his content-creators: a crew of seven boys who were committed to becoming South Korea's next K-Pop idols. RM, Suga, and J-hope were the original three and Jin, Jimin, V, and Jungkook were added as audition-worthy candidates.

So, what type of content did Bang hope that BTS would create? As he explains with a knowing smile, "The moment when 'a content' becomes 'good content' is the moment where 'unique' turns 'universal' and resonates with someone's soul."

The charter of BTS' music-creation was rooted in dichotomy: it had to be both universal enough to capture an audience, while also being niche enough to generate a passionate response from a specific group of followers.[374]

The key example of this phenomenon is in the case of comic books. In the 1960s and 1970s, comic-based superheroes were a niche genre only liked by the comic mania. However, the enthusiasm of that group and universality of the content has birthed a resurgence in re-purposing superhero content in new forms like high-grossing movies, books, or television series. What once used to be niche Marvel comics has now grossed over $22.5 billion worldwide in theaters.[375] Good content, as Bang describes, must make a statement in the era it exists, while remaining universal and appealing to specific groups of people.

In the YouTube era, BTS has mastered the creation of universal, contemporary, follower-specific, and passionate content. It's the reason why Bang insists that BTS members write and compose their own music rather than hiring this out to "experts." However, content is only one part of the equation; BTS also thrived in identifying a market and fitting their content into an international growth engine of opportunity.

THE MARKET (& ITS FIT)

The first few years of BTS was filled with failure after failure after failure. On debut in June 2013, their first album (with their first track "No More Dream") sold a total of nineteen thousand units.[376] Bang had chartered the boys to talk about issues that young people experience, especially since they were young kids at the time. Despite pouring their emotions into the writing, their next two albums (O!RUL8,2? and Skool Luv Affair) didn't fair too much better either. Even though Skool Luv Affair charted at number three in the Billboard World charts, even the internal BTS team didn't see it as a large accomplishment.[377]

It wasn't until August 2014 when BTS released "Dark & Wild" that their future started to look up. They sold 100,000 copies and were invited to attend KCON in LA to perform at one of the largest fan celebrations of Korean culture and music. As Bang Si Hyuk recalls,

The way in which the audience was reacting to BTS was different from what we had seen before for K-Pop acts in the US.[378]

By the next year, BTS released "I Need You" and received their first music show win ever.

Perhaps it's worth pausing here and asking an obvious question: How did BTS, a totally novel group, even get invited to a global performance and break into the global scene after just one year? As Im Zin-Mo, a popular South Korean music critic, reflects,

BTS was successful in the global stage because of a different strategy. Most idol groups secured some recognition and market share domestically before going abroad. But BTS aimed to go overseas right from the group's 2013 debut.[379]

In fact, in their first two years alone, BTS conducted four world tours spanning North America, Europe, South America, and Asia (Thailand, Japan, etc.) to expand their presence and meet fans face-to-face. Even when they weren't physically traveling, BTS engaged with international fans through television shows and talk shows for niche K-Pop fans like the *After School Club*.

With memorable performances (some of which take more than twelve hours of rehearsal a day), an endearing charisma across the seven boys, and genuine engagement via individual social media accounts, the members of BTS created a community of fans rather than a base of consumers. They shared their most raw moments, experiences, and photos with the world in a way that made the average fan feel part of the boys' friendship and success. Rather than creating a content media strategy, Bang sought to create a genuine aura of camaraderie between the BTS boys to attract passionate fans. This too is a strategy that Bang took with the group from day one:

When I met them before BTS was planned, honestly, I was not able to even dream of such a future that is their present right now. "I need to make them into international artists!" I have never set such a goal before. All BTS members were young students who suddenly came up to Seoul from the provinces. Our company wasn't seen as what was so-called "mainstream" either. But I was confident in one thing: it was the confidence that I will make something meaningful happen with these friends who possess brilliant talents.[380]

Ultimately, this friendship between band members also led to a deep friendship and relationship between the fans. BTS fans call themselves the ARMY, or "Adorable Representative M.C. for Youth." While the ARMY started small, its grown to have millions of members. In 2020 alone, there were eighteen million unique authors mentioning BTS online. As Brand-watch cheekily commented in January 2021, "If BTS fans were to form a real army (of one million men and women), there would be enough people for at least eighteen armies".[381]

Seeing the growth of their global fanbase and the excitement that fans had while interacting with BTS, Bang intentionally decided to create a US-focused album release. Using fans as a marketing engine, their album "Wings" debuted in 2016 at number twenty-six on the Billboard 200, a tough feat con-sidering there weren't many non-Western artists on the list at all. Fueled by success, they went on their second world tour and immediately released two back-to-back number one Billboard 200 albums "Love Yourself: Tear" and "Love Yourself: Answer," a first for BTS and for the K-Pop scene as a whole.[382] Their third world tour, unsurprisingly, was a series of sold-out stadiums night after night in 2018. As the band reflects, it was at this point that they began to realize the power of the ARMY.[383]

In addition to creating primary content fit to the BTS ARMY market (a primary motivation for the first three years of their business), BTS has excelled in inspiring their fans to cre-ate secondary content. BTS fans create K-Pop clubs at their schools where they relearn the groups dances, pay $22-150 per year for exclusive membership fan clubs, and even translate BTS songs or speeches into new languages.[384] The distribu-tion that BTS is able to reach as a result of their content-mar-ket fit is truly viral: every fan infects a few others with their love of BTS and a few super-spreaders help to keep the BTS fever alive with significant investments in the community.

Given that BTS did not have the support or resources of any of the big three entertainment firms, it is actually quite impressive what Bang has been able to achieve. They piggybacked off the new social media technologies in 2013 and developed their own, unique fan-based playbook for developing a flywheel of fan engagement. BTS engages with fans on Twitter, YouTube, and other social media platforms (either directly or through "secret content" like behind the scenes videos); fans become excited and engage with the BTS ARMY; the BTS ARMY influences how BTS creates content; and the whole virtuous cycle continues. As we can learn from how Bang designed BTS, true content market fit is a constant ping between fans, engagement, content, and adaptation.

In listening to BTS interviews, it's striking that all seven band members thank the ARMY. Even as they interview about winning awards such as South Korea's first Billboard music award or charting as number one on Billboard's hot 100 global list, the band is clear about the importance of their genuine content and its fit in improving the lives of their fans.

Achieving number one on the Billboard Hot 100: it's kind of like, although we recently got nominated for a Grammy the feeling of getting number one on Billboard Hot 100 is different because the Billboard Hot 100 is inclusive of all worldwide music. And the fact that we got number one made me think that our music, our sincerity, is touching so many people. Realizing that, we are reaching people and really connecting with them. I think that was the most meaningful part. This wasn't the album we had planned out, yet this happened.[385]

BTS has seen extreme success on social media. As of February 2021, they had 37.6 million Instagram followers, 44 million YouTube subscribers, and 32.5M Twitter followers on their official account. When aggregating their individual accounts, this number nears almost 100 million. For context, artists like Justin Bieber, Beyonce, and Drake have 163 million, 116 million, and 76 million followers respectively. This fandom is an engine of success that will pave the way for the future of K-Pop.

As Bang reflects with a content smile and reflection,

The situation right now even after thirty years has passed is similar (to the 1970s–1980s). It's a reality that there aren't many countries that are able to impose their own country's musical characteristics. In most countries around the world, people are still mainly consuming US-centric Pop music. However, in the present 2018, for us, we have K-Pop. Even up until the early 2000s, I didn't think that K-Pop would be able to have a global position. However, many leading entertainment companies and senior artists didn't give up, repeating lots of tries and starting to pave the road. The result of that is that the present K-Pop extended beyond Korea ad came to be recognized by the public around the world.[386]

The key to beating the odds and unlocking the Big Hit Entertainment Unicorn lies in understanding the content-market fit that BTS achieved to fuel exponential growth through their fans rather than traditional television-based media platforms. BTS' content is genuine and reflects relatable human beings while appealing to a once niche audience of the BTS ARMY and their market loves their content and music, which is not only relatable but constantly fresh as well. The big bang behind BTS is Bang himself.

Chapter Summary

Lesson 1. Even though only 20 percent of the world speaks English, more than 70 percent of the world's most popular streamed music is in English. K-Pop (pop music originating in Korea) is slowly changing this statistic. While most Westerners were first exposed to K-Pop through PSY's "Gangnam Style" the history of K-Pop starts in 1992. In the last thirty years, K-Pop groups have spitted and sputtered but none have caught fire quite as much as BTS. The group is estimated to have brought more than $3.6 billion to the South Korean economy in 2018 and as of January 2021 had been nominated for over 500 national and international music awards. They've broken world records and gained global prominence. Their success, in large part, relies on the execution strategy of billionaire and group founder Bang Si-Hyuk (aka Hitman, aka Bang PD).

Lesson 2. While recruiting K-Pop idols, Bang focused on finding trainees who loved music for its own sake: not for the thrills and frills. Despite this noble cause, the business almost failed until Bang and his team derived two key insights: (1) Most entertainment companies do not effectively use technology to pull people together and (2) while idols are important, the most crucial part of success for any media business are the fans.

Lesson 3. For technology businesses looking to scale, one of the key insights that entrepreneurs attempt to achieve is "product-market fit." Trying to align one's product to strong market demand by releasing products, acquiring feedback, and tweaking products. BTS adopted a similar approach by focusing on "content-market fit." They developed great content that could be tested and tweaked through social media engagement with fans. The BTS ARMY is a necessary component of the story behind Bang's innovation because they allow a feedback mechanism for creating music with massive appeal.

CONCLUSION

———

Ralph Clark is the child of a single mom. Born as a Black boy in the 1960s in Oakland, California, nothing in his background would have hinted at his future success. As we were chatting through LED screens, his jovial smile and demeanor lit up my laptop and set me at ease.

"What's one thing you still have from your childhood?" I asked to start our conversation.

Optimism. That's a thing I have from my childhood. I was always a very optimistic child for whatever reason, and I continue to be incredibly optimistic even as an older adult.[387]

For forty-five minutes, we explored this optimism and where it came from. I peeled the onion to understand what Ralph learned while attending parochial schools, attending Harvard for an MBA as the first in his family to go to college, and eventually being a C-suite executive at seven different companies.

Ralph has had an envious career. In the last three decades, he has run and sold four companies to acquirers like Ask Jeeves,

WebMD, Upshot, and Symantec. He now runs ShotSpotter, a surveillance technology that detects, locates, and alerts law enforcement of outdoor gunshot activity.

By the traditional American model, Ralph is a success. And when tracing Ralph's journey there is no denying the Unlocking Unicorns framework of exploration, refinement, and execution that he applied to his life.

Ralph is an example of Black excellence.

Despite growing up in the midst of the civil rights movement, he is a Black CEO of a publicly traded company in a world where being Black and a prominent CEO is still extremely rare. In fact, since the Fortune 500 list was published in 1955 there have only been nineteen Black CEOs out of 1,800 chief executives.[388] Perhaps what's more striking is that there have been more chief executives named John in the history of this list than there have been Black executives.

Just as Ralph made his career in America at a time of social change, we are in the midst of a global movement toward equity and equality.

The world is changing.

The last fifty years will not look like the next fifty years.

Everyday entrepreneurs in Africa, Asia, and the Middle East are starting enterprises that will become the next multi-million-dollar businesses. Some may even be Unicorn companies with valuations of a billion dollars or more.

As a potential startup founder, investor, or advisor in the next century, it's important to remember that the inspiration and intelligence for great companies can come from anyone, anywhere. Just as innovation came from a Black boy in Oakland fifty years ago.

Growing up as a Ghanaian American, I loved the startup stories of Bill Gates, Jeff Bezos, and Steve Jobs. However, as I continued to see only white men featured in startup legends, I began to ask myself: *Is there a place for me in this industry?* Ralph is one example of a diverse wave of executives in business who have influenced and continue to influence business today. This book is a small sliver of evidence that novel lessons about building Unicorn companies can come from the "third-world" (a term that I find demeaning for the people who live there).

Emerging economies have emerging insights that can't be found anywhere else.

This book includes only a fraction of successful non-Western Unicorns based in emerging economies. However, I believe that by the end of this decade we will need a full library to house all the lessons learned and stories shared. And believe me when I tell you that this book is just the beginning of a personal journey to catalog and learn each and every anecdote.

It's not a question of *if* or even a question of *when* companies in emerging economies will dominate the world, but one of "*how.*"

How will the Western world adapt to the rise of Unicorn companies in the developing world? In nearly every region discussed in this book, internet usage is growing, population is booming, and small-to medium-sized businesses are flourishing. The ripple effects of these changes will continue to build the infrastructures and opportunities of countries overlooked in the last century. Moreover, these countries will begin to produce technologies that leap-frog those in the West. Already, companies like TikTok or Taobao Live have become the envious copycat targets of today's largest American tech companies. The lessons and insights from these institutions as teased out in this book offer tips for building differentiated businesses.

How will investors choose to allocate their capital to start-ups in the next decade? While the West (America, Canada, and the UK) will continue to have break-out Unicorn companies, these deals continue to become more and more expensive. In more matured countries, the price to play only increases. As an investor, where would you rather put your money? Into an industry nearing its prime or one that's just beginning?

How will entrepreneurs in Africa, the Middle East, and Asia build their companies? In this book I offered a few tips with stories from ten startup legends of different archetypes who have done it before.

In Part 1, you learned about three individuals who explored in order to find and operate their businesses. Jack Ma is a poster child of failure. But he's masterful at *strategic* failure by taking losses and finding ways to network or learn his way into wins in the future. Kiran Mazumdar-Shaw broke every mold as a contrarian to become the only female self-made billionaire in India. She's evidence that anti-conformity can actually be an asset, especially as a woman in a male-dominated industry or country. And finally, Mitchell Elegbe demonstrated that discernment and viewing the world with different hues can lead to ground-breaking insights. These three explorers broke ground in the emerging world.

In Part 2, I shared four stories of founders who effectively refined the mass of ideas and strategies floating in their heads to develop a crystal-clear plan for implementation. Mudassir Sheikha was a maestro in using a keen North Star of belief to create a business that benefits the broader ecosystem in the Middle East and North Africa while also developing local talent. Cher Wang was able to reframe her many career paths and familial pressures to create a business and life that went against the odds. She reframed problems and relationships to ensure her business success. Third, the team at Andela took what is often seen as a weakness (diverse talent from diverse backgrounds) to create a strength (unity, teamwork, and a mosaic of cooperation). This shift was all enabled by a refined mission to uplift software developers across Africa. And fourth, Robin Li was able to pivot his business and life from a research focus to a practical endeavor. After many attempts, eventually, one of these pivots led to business model changes and product changes that are still bearing fruit today.

Then in Part 3, you discovered three powerhouse executors. Once they had explored ideas and refined to one, they poured gasoline on the fire to create a rocket ship. Blitzscaling to success. Ritesh Agarwal used his unrelenting ambition to push the bar for himself and his team higher and higher. In addition to his regret minimization frameworks, he inspired his team to have similar ambitions. Hooi Ling Tan realized that in a fragmented ecosystem like Southeast Asia, the most important requirement is a partnership-first approach. This mindset opened doors that would otherwise have been closed to startups. And third, Bang Si-hyuk executed exceptionally through fan-creation and fan-feedback to turn a business opportunity of seven Korean boys into a billion-dollar opportunity.

Each founder, though different in how they achieved success, share in their ability to unlock a Unicorn. Building a business of $1 billion or more is no small feat, but one overarching theme is the risk each took to take a bet on themselves. As a result, the names of the businesses (and their founders) will go down in history: Alibaba, Biocon, Interswitch, Careem, HTC, Andela, Baidu, OYO, Grab, and BTS.

So, what does this all mean for you? As a citizen of an emerging economy, this book is a rallying cry with examples of why and how you can do it. As a citizen of a developed nation, this book is a guidebook for finding the next set of companies to invest resources. As a citizen of the world, this book is a glimpse into the future.

No matter who you are, discover, consume, and share the stories of underrepresented founders. The world is shaped by those who act.

Unlock the Unicorns in everyone around you.

ACKNOWLEDGMENTS

In the midst of a global pandemic, which forced everyone home, I set out on a journey to change the narrative of entrepreneurship. A successful founder can be any color and can come from anywhere. But collecting these stories and distilling them into a narrative has not been easy. First, I'd like to thank and acknowledge the first founders in my life: Mommy, Daddy, Rachel, and Joel. Together, in starting "Hugs for _" fifteen years ago, you taught me that a startup can both do good and be profitable. Not to mention, you've always been there through all my shenanigans and encouraged me as I quarantined in my childhood bedroom to write. I love you!

To create this book, I had dozens of conversations with founders, emerging economy experts, and operators around the world. Each taught me something new and gave me a chance to explore my passion for international development through entrepreneurship. A special thank you to every single person mentioned in this book, regardless of context, for being a part of my life and for teaching me something valuable.

I also wanted to give a very special thank you to everyone from all walks of my life who supported my early drafts of this book through their time (being a beta reader), talent (connecting me to relevant individuals), and treasurer (purchasing a pre-sale copy). I am forever grateful for and to you all: Ayushi Sinha, Henri Pierre-Jacques, Jarrid Tingle, Lauren Lee, Janet Chen, Kash Goudarzi, Oliver Collins, Diego Rejtman, Leora Huebner, Kathryn Nunes, Nicholas Stager, Jared Cohen, Meera Rajagopalan, Brandon Hoffman, Naily Nevarez, David Lemson, Eric Koester, Yehong Zhu, Jan Philip Petershagen, Anthony Amihere, Shemiele Fikru, Mutesa Sithole, Ahmed Elsayyad, Jessica Li, Arjun Naik, Ronia Hurwitz, Herve Kibala, Karim Abdou, Joel Kwartler, Kristen Hong, Aneesh Rastogi, Liam McGregor, Jay Li, Andrew Tawaststjerna, Elizabeth Petrov, Ritvik Salim, Frances Ling, Jesse Shulman, Michael Smith, Sophia Saenz, Dae Durisko, Erik Schluntz, William Roller, Aaron Dibble, Jared Lang, Ryan Bloomer, Bayard Blair, Rachel Brown, Kelly Charlton, Rosamond Lu, Daniel Dippold, Lynn E Thompson, Katherine Choi, Ben Magbual, Karen Albert, Pat Boonyarittipong, Frank Pacheco, Dan LaBruna, Marci Zainwel, Anant Pai, Cecil Williams II, Lan Kim, Alexis Wheeler, Bobby Vavassis, Stephen Shurtleff, Michael I. Norton, Serena Hagerty, Grace Cormier, David Levari, Ximena Garcia-Rada, Shannon Sciarappa, Hanne Collins, Brandon Ko, Emily Prinsloo, Alexander Walsh, Abdelwadood Daoud, Juliana Tioanda, Mary Gao, CC Gleser, Abdul Jamjoom, Jimin Nam, Danny Sheridan, Houston Kraft, Eana Meng, Gaurav Uppal, Carli Stein, Simi Shah, Christopher Datsikas, Jake Hughson, Bryan Stelling, Ed Luera, Naushard Cader, Angela Marith, Verena Conley, Derek Hu, Carson D. Sweezy, John Vela, Patrick Lyons, Devina Singh, Kathleen Malloch, Rachel Greenwald,

Edmond Dankyi, Jillian Kraker, Todd Baldwin, Alexandra Foote, Rahul Surti, Tom Vollmer, Jack Huang, Hehe Shen, Lital Levy, Amara Anigbo, Charlotte Lewis, Drew Reid, Bill Cho, Stephen Turban, Stephen Harper, Akporesiri Omene, Ashka Stephen, Gautham Reddy, Dilraj Devgun, Anastacia Cervantes, James Kim, Brian Lai, Palak Goel, Jackson Crewe, Francis Abugbilla, Timothy Lann, MJ Allen, Annie Zhao, Spencer Jamison, Nathan Gupta, Vanessa Alix, Kai Cash, Adam Coccari, Larry McEvoy, Osazuwa George Okpamen, Noel Rivard, Amy Bell, Jonathan King, Sophie Jewsbury, Flora DiCara, Riley Soward, Lucy Bennett-Baggs, Philip Ruffini, Daniel Belfort, Derek DaSilva, Katherine Wang, Olivia Kim, Alp Aysan, Christine Hong, Christina Li, Natalie Purcell, Beth Morin, and Paul Lei.

Finally, I would like to thank God for giving me the strength, inspiration, and wisdom to share these thoughts with the world.

APPENDIX

———

INTRODUCTION

Alspach, Kyle. "Hubspot Plots New Acquisitions, Says Performable Cost $20m." *Boston Business Journal,* September 19, 2012. https://www. bizjournals.com/boston/blog/startups/2012/09/hubspot-acquisitions-performable-cost.html.

Campbell, John. "Last Month, Over Half-a-Billion Africans Accessed the Internet." *Council on Foreign Relations,* July 2019. https://www. cfr.org/blog/last-month-over-half-billion-africans-accessed-internet.

China Power Team. "How Web-Connected Is China?" China Power, April 18, 2019. Updated August 25, 2020. Accessed February 21, 2021. https:// chinapower.csis.org/web-connectedness/.

Kaka, Noshir, Anu Madgavkar, Alok Kshirsagar, Rajat Gupta, James Manyika, Kushe Bahl, Shishir Gupta. "Digital India: Technology to Transform a Connected Nation." *McKinsey Global Institute,* March 2019. https://www.mckinsey.com/~/media/McKinsey/Business%20 Functions/McKinsey%20Digital/Our%20Insights/Digital%20 India%20Technology%20to%20transform%20a%20connected%20 nation/MGI-Digital-India-Report-April-2019.pdf.

"This Startling Graph Shows How Many Africans Are Now Using the Internet - Far More Than in North America, And on Track to Beat Europe." *Business Insider South Africa,* July 24, 2019. https://www.businessinsider.co.za/internet-users-in-africa-2019-7.

Torres, Elias. "More Equity: Elias Torres of Drift." Interview with Michael Bervell. *Harlem Capital More Equity Podcast.* Podcast Audio, October 2020, https://open.spotify.com/episode/oBIZoD1b9AVIB1wUcMYX-NP?si=PJYb_1XlSpeFwvTYPy8Rrw.

"U.S. Department of State." Accessed February 21, 2021. https://travel.state.gov/content/travel/en/about-us/reports-and-statistics.html.

CHAPTER 1: 1,001 FAILURES

All-Russian Science Festival. "Jack Ma (Alibaba Group, AliExpress) at Lomonosov Moscow State University." May 5, 2019. Video, 1:03:52. https://www.youtube.com/watch?v=g25jcvtjZjA.

Belli, Gina. "How Many Jobs Are Found Through Networking, Really?" *PayScale,* April 6, 2017. https://www.payscale.com/career-news/2017/04/many-jobs-found-networking.

CNBCAfrica. "Alibaba's Jack Ma's Lessons for African Entrepreneurs." August 15, 2018. Video, 26:29. https://www.youtube.com/watch?v=LToLyCgozeI.

CNBC International TV. "Jack Ma, Founder of Alibaba | The Brave Ones." October 13, 2017. Video, 25:44. https://www.youtube.com/watch?v=A-HoIfJDRQ7M.

Farnam, T.W. "Study Shows Revolving Door of Employment between Congress, Lobbying Firms." *Washington Post,* September 13, 2011. https://www.washingtonpost.com/study-shows-revolving-door-of-employment-between-congress-lobbying-firms/2011/09/12/gIQAx-PYROK_story.html.

Gage, Deborah. "The Venture Capital Secret: 3 Out of 4 Start-Ups Fail." *Wall Street Journal,* September 20, 2012. https://www.wsj.com/articles/SB10000872396390443720204578004980476429190.

Gompers, Paul A., Anna Kovner, Josh Lerner, and David S. Scharfstein. "Performance Persistence in Entrepreneurship." *Harvard Business School Working Paper,* no 09-028 (September 2008).https://www.hbs.edu/faculty/Publication%20Files/09-028.pdf.

Gottschalk, Sandra, Francis J. Greene, Daniel Höwer, and Bettina Müller, "If You Don't Succeed, Should You Try Again? The Role of Entrepreneurial Experience in Venture Survival." *ZEW Discussion Paper,* no. 14-009, (2014). https://www.cambridge.org/core/journals/management-and-organization-review/article/chinese-entrepreneurs-social-networks-and-guanxi/43CF75DF8F6CDF6EF8047C2566F091AE.

Harvard Business School. "Admissions Class of 2022 Profile." Accessed January 14, 2021. https://www.hbs.edu/mba/admissions/class-profile/Pages/default.aspx.

Jack Ma. Crocodile in the Yangtze Full - Story of Alibaba & Jack Ma Full Documentary. October 24, 2015. Video, 1:17:03. https://www.youtube.com/watch?v=RkVJNOQ7B74.

NTV Kenya, "Jack Ma's Full Public Lecture at the University of Nairobi." July 20, 2017, Video, 38:42. https://www.youtube.com/watch?v=IEkT-YatPnM.

Reynolds, Paul. "Worldwide Business Start-Ups," *MKM Research,* 2017. http://www.moyak.com/papers/business-startups-entrepreneurs.html.

Soontorn Sri-on. "Conversation with Jack Ma." October 11, 2016. Video, 3:03:54. https://www.youtube.com/watch?v=24Nmrwv8isg.

Stanford Graduate School of Business. "Alibaba's Ma Reflects on 12-Year Journey at China 2.0 Conference." October 5, 2011. Video, 56:47. https://www.youtube.com/watch?v=ZH9-_GLqGC4.

Stanford Graduate School of Business, "Jack Ma, Alibaba Group: Stanford GSB 2015 Entrepreneurial Company of the Year." September 30, 2015. Video, 1:08:04. https://www.youtube.com/watch?v=kh_wPWQrWZA.

Startup Genome, "Global Startup Ecosystem Report 2019." Accessed January 15, 2021. https://startupgenome.com/.

Statista, "Alibaba Group - Statistics & Facts." Last modified June 9, 2020. Accessed November 10, 2020. https://www.statista.com/topics/2187/alibaba-group/.

Wenderoth, Michael. "How A Better Understanding of Guanxi Can Improve Your Business in China." *Forbes,* May 16, 2018. https://www.forbes.com/sites/michaelcwenderoth/2018/05/16/how-a-better-understanding-of-guanxi-can-improve-your-business-in-china/?sh=648547815d85.

CHAPTER 2: CONTRARIAN CHALLENGER

Armstrong, Lance. "The 2010 Time 100: Kiran Mazumdar-Shaw," *Time,* April 29, 2010. http://content.time.com/time/specials/packages/article/0,28804,1984685_1984949_1985233,00.html.

Business Wire. "Number of Women-Owned Businesses Growing 2.5 Times Faster Than National Average." *Business Insider,* November 8, 2017. https://markets.businessinsider.com/news/stocks/number-of-women-owned-businesses-growing-2-5-times-faster-than-national-average-1007300927.

ENDEVR. "How Entrepreneur Kiran Mazumdar-Shaw Created an Empire | High Flyers | ENDEVR Documentary." September 23, 2020. Video, 23:51. https://www.youtube.com/watch?v=vLB45SgX6zI.

Financial Times. "Kiran Mazumdar-Shaw." Accessed December 28, 2020. https://www.ft.com/content/afd4093a-ed9b-11df-9085-00144feab49a.

Forbes. "#727 Kiran Mazumdar-Shaw." Accessed December 29, 2020. https://www.forbes.com/profile/kiran-mazumdar-shaw/?sh=3a33a7c59ad7.

Her Power. "Her Power: Kiran Mazumdar Shaw." October 19, 2015. Video, 11:39. https://www.youtube.com/watch?v=G-fpFabqgd4.

Lesonsky, Rieva. "The State of Women Entrepreneurs." *Score,* March 24, 2020. https://www.score.org/blog/state-women-entrepreneurs.

Mazumdar-Shaw, Kiran. "Kiran Mazumdar-Shaw Says She Has Inherited Her Independent Streak from Her Mother." *The Economic Times,* March 8, 2020. https://economictimes.indiatimes.com/magazines/panache/kiran-mazumdar-shaw-says-she-has-inherited-her-independent-streak-from-her-mother/articleshow/74532052.cms.

"More Than 250m Women Worldwide Are Entrepreneurs, According to the Global Entrepreneurship Monitor Women's Report from Babson College and Smith College." *PR Newswire,* November 18, 2019. https://www.prnewswire.com/news-releases/more-than-250m-women-worldwide-are-entrepreneurs-according-to-the-global-entrepreneurship-monitor-womens-report-from-babson-college-and-smith-college-300960196.html.

Myers, David G. "The Social Animal." In *Rethinking Human Nature: A Multidisciplinary Approach,* edited by Malcolm A. Jeeves, 206-223. Grand Rapids: William B. Eerdmans Pub. Company, 2010. https://www3.nd.edu/~rwilliam/xsoc530/conformity.html.

Sadhguru. "Kiran Mazumdar-Shaw in Conversation with Sadhguru, 2017." April 29, 2017. Video, 1:33:07. https://www.youtube.com/watch?v=vR2CclEUVco.

Saha, Devanik. "Women Run 14% of Indian Businesses, Most Self-Financed." *The Wire,* May 7, 2016. https://thewire.in/gender/women-run-14-of-indian-businesses-most-self-financed.

Sameer Hashmi. "Kiran Mazumdar Shaw Interview—BBC News." October 9, 2018. Video, 15:45. https://www.youtube.com/watch?v=P3vCS-f8bHZs.

Science History Institute. "Women in Chemistry: Kiran Mazumdar-Shaw." February 1, 2013. Video, 17:42. https://www.youtube.com/watch?v=PtbN2ky7Ffo.

Snyder, Benjamin. "7 Insights from Legendary Investor Warren Buffett." *CNBC,* May 1, 2017. https://www.cnbc.com/2017/05/01/7-insights-from-legendary-investor-warren-buffett.html.

Teare, Gené. "Global VC Funding to Female Founders Dropped Dramatically This Year." *Crunchbase News,* December 21, 2020. https://news.crunchbase.com/news/global-vc-funding-to-female-founders/.

Tingle, Jarrid. "If You Do Average Things." *LinkedIn,* January 2021. https://www.linkedin.com/posts/jarrid-tingle_if-you-do-average-things-expect-average-activity-6747932818527068160-uCOa.

"Who Am I? By Meet Kamani: Dr. Kiran Mazumdar Shaw." Accessed December 28, 2020. https://sites.google.com/site/whoamibymeetkamani/women-entrepreneurs/dr-kiran-mazumdar-shaw.

World Bank Group. "Working for Women in India." Accessed December 28, 2020. https://www.worldbank.org/en/news/feature/2019/03/08/working-for-women-in-india.

CHAPTER 3: SANGUINE SEER

Adeshokan, Oluwatosin. "Toyota Is Making a Small Bet on a Big Opportunity in African Mobility Startups." *Quartz Africa,* February 5, 2020. https://qz.com/africa/1797709/toyota-bets-on-african-mobility-startup-sendy-in-kenya/.

Biz Watch Nigeria. "Verve Marks 10th Anniversary." October 12, 2019. Video, 23:50. https://www.youtube.com/watch?v=mwMe9ikcBqY.

Bright, Jake. "Interswitch CEO Mitchell Elegbe to Discuss African Fintech at TechCrunch Disrupt." *TechCrunch,* September 8, 2020. https://techcrunch.com/2020/09/08/interswitch-ceo-mitchell-elegbe-to-discuss-african-fintech-at-techcrunch-disrupt/.

Bright, Jake. "Nigeria's Interswitch Confirms $1b Valuation after Visa Investment." *TechCrunch,* November 11, 2019. https://techcrunch.com/2019/11/11/nigerias-interswitch-confirms-1b-valuation-after-visa-investment/.

Costa, James. "How Jack Ma Sees a Thriving Future of Entrepreneurship in Africa." *World Economic Forum,* March 2, 2020. https://www.weforum.org/agenda/2020/03/jack-ma-alibaba-digital-entrepreneurship-africa/.

Hattingh, Damian, Acha Leke, and Bill Russo. "Lions (Still) On the Move: Growth in Africa's Consumer Sector." *McKinsey,* October 2, 2017. https://www.mckinsey.com/industries/consumer-packaged-goods/our-insights/lions-still-on-the-move-growth-in-africas-consumer-sector.

Heeralall, Nirmal and Raoudha Ben Abdelkrim. "The World's Fastest-Growing Middle Class." *UHY.* Accessed February 20, 2021. http://www.uhy.com/the-worlds-fastest-growing-middle-class/.

Henry, Nzekwe. "Unpacking the Untold Story behind the Company That Is Set to Become Nigeria's First Billion-Dollar Tech Firm." *WeeTracker,* November 11, 2019. https://weetracker.com/2019/11/11/interswitch-is-set-for-unicorn-status/.

Hinds, Rebecca. "Three Defining Trends in Corporate Venture Capital Right Now." *Affinity.* Accessed June 11, 2021. https://www.affinity.co/blog/corporate-venture-capital-trends.

Igwenagu, Emmanuel. "Mitchell Elegbe: The Man Behind Multi-Billion Dollars Payment Solution Infrastructure, Interswitch." *Nigerian Informer,* December 17, 2019. https://nigerianinformer.com/mitchell-elegbe-the-man-behind-multi-billion-dollars-payment-solution-infrastructure-interswitch/.

"Interswitch and Visa Enter into Strategic Partnership." *Visa*, December 11, 2019. https://www.visa.co.za/about-visa/newsroom/press-releases/prl-12112019.html.

InterswitchSPAK. "Interswitchspak2.0 Season Finale: Closing Remarks by Mitchell Elegbe, Interswitch Founder and GMD." February 8, 2020. Video, 16:55. https://www.youtube.com/watch?v=nxB0ti8Vbxk.

LABS by ARM. "Why Startup Capital is Necessary, But not Sufficient - Mitchell Elegbe." May 6, 2020. Video, 1:29:53. https://www.youtube.com/watch?v=_tKX9w50eWU.

Lagos Business School. "Define Your Future with Mitchell Elegbe - Group CEO, Interswitch." August 10, 2019. Video, 7:38. https://www.youtube.com/watch?v=T12JhmjzquE.

Liivak, Mattias. "Infographic: What Are the Top 10 Cash-Based Economies of the World?" *Fortumo*, June 2, 2015. https://fortumo.com/blog/what-are-the-top-10-cash-based-economies-of-the-world/.

"Mitchell Elegbe: A Life of Possibilities." *SPICE Nigeria*. March 26, 2008. https://ilovespicemagazine.wordpress.com/2008/03/26/mitchell-elegbe-a-life-of-possibilities/.

"Mitchell Elegbe: Meet Visionary Who Transformed Epayments in Nigeria." *Technology Times*, December 23, 2020. https://technologytimes.ng/mitchell-elegbe-meet-visionary-transformed-epayments-in-nigeria/.

National Youth Service Corps - NYSC. "About the NYSC Scheme." Accessed February 7, 2021. https://www.nysc.gov.ng/.

Nwoye, Chidinma Irene. "African Countries Are Seeing a 'Brain Gain' as Young Elite Graduates Give Up on the West." *Quartz Africa*, November 24, 2017. https://qz.com/africa/1128778/africa-brain-drain-to-brain-gain-african-elite-graduates-head-home-as-brexit-trump-eu-close-doors/.

Onukwue, Alexander. "For the First Time, Around 100 African Startups Raise At Least $1 Million Each in One Year." *Techcabal*, January 9, 2020. https://techcabal.com/2020/01/09/for-the-first-time-around-100-african-startups-raise-at-least-1-million-in-one-year/.

Pocket World in Figures 2020. England: Economist Books, 2019.

Statista, "Countries with the Highest Population in 1950, 2013, 2050, And 2100." Last modified December 2, 2014. Accessed February 20, 2021. https://www.statista.com/statistics/268107/countries-with-the-highest-population/.

Statista, "Fertility Rate in Nigeria from 2008 to 2018." Last modified March 31, 2021. Accessed February 20, 2021. https://www.statista.com/statistics/382212/fertility-rate-in-nigeria/.

Statista, "GDP of African Countries 2020, by Country." Last Modified February 18, 2021. Accessed February 20, 2021. https://www.statista.com/statistics/1120999/gdp-of-african-countries-by-country/.

Statista, "Share of Payments with E-wallet in Nigeria in 2020, By Leading Service." Last modified October 22, 2020. Accessed February 20, 2021. https://www.statista.com/statistics/1175909/share-of-payments-with-e-wallet-in-nigeria/.

Statista, "United States: Fertility Rate from 2008 to 2018." Last modified March 31, 2021. Accessed February 20, 2021. https://www.statista.com/statistics/269941/fertility-rate-in-the-us/.

TC Video. "Making Bank." September 16, 2020. Video. https://techcrunch.com/video/making-bank/.

TEDx Talks. "What Do You See: Mitchell Elegbe at TEDxVictoriaIsland." November 10, 2012. Video, 17:53. https://www.youtube.com/watch?v=vR8QFiZ4ACc.

The Banker. "Interview with Mitchell Elegbe, CEO of Interswitch." October 22, 2013. Video, 7:41. https://www.youtube.com/watch?v=x-KXO3Q_eyMA.

The Bridge Leadership Foundation. "9th Career Day - Technology and Innovation: Opportunities, Challenges and the Future." July 13, 2020. Video, 1:10:13. https://www.youtube.com/watch?v=VlWhBs1w4as.

The World Bank. "Nigeria at-a-Glance." Accessed February 7, 2021. https://www.worldbank.org/en/country/nigeria.

WeeTracker Team, "African Venture Capital 2018 Report – USD 725.6 Mn Invested in 458 Deals." WeeTracker, January 4, 2019. https://www.weetracker.com/2019/01/04/what-a-year-the-state-of-venture-capital-in-africa-2018/.

PART 2: REFINEMENT AND ENCHIRIDION

Experian, "Student Loan Debt Reaches Record High as Most Repayment Is Paused." Accessed June 7, 2021. https://www.experian.com/blogs/ask-experian/state-of-student-loan-debt/.

Oxford Dictionaries, s.v. "Enchiridion," accessed June 7, 2021. https://www.lexico.com/definition/enchiridion.

CHAPTER 4: THE ABCS

Ahmed, Masood. "Youth Unemployment in the MENA Region: Determinants and Challenges." *International Monetary Fund,* June 2012. https://www.imf.org/external/np/vc/2012/061312.htm?id=186569.

Careem. "Our Story." Accessed January 2021. https://www.careem.com/en-ae/our-story/.

Careem. "Taking on the Big Boys and Winning - Rise Conference 2018." July 23, 2018. Video, 25:35. https://www.youtube.com/watch?v=e5G-2GyitRIQ.

Chen, James and Gordon Scott. "Middle East and North Africa (MENA)." *Investopedia,* May 20, 2021. https://www.investopedia.com/terms/m/middle-east-and-north-africa-mena.asp#.

Dhal, Sharmila. "Ramadan Kareem or Ramadan Mubarak?" *Gulf News,* March 28, 2020. https://gulfnews.com/uae/ramadan-kareem-or-ramadan-mubarak-1.63755186.

Endeavor Jordan. "Mudassir Sheikha - DealMakers 2016 Keynote Talk." December 2, 2016. Video, 1:04:06. https://www.youtube.com/watch?v=6sP3-ZePptg.

FastCompany. "Careem." Accessed January 2021. https://www.fastcompany.com/company/careem.

GX: Government Experience. "Mudassir Sheikha - CEO of Careem - GXTalks JAN 31 FullSession." February 5, 2019. Video, 39:03. https://www.youtube.com/watch?v=fgJuagSrMjc.

Haddad, Carmen. "Bridging the Female Unemployment Gap in MENA – The Role of the Private Sector." *Business Chief,* May 19, 2020. https://www.businesschief.eu/leadership-and-strategy/bridging-female-unemployment-gap-mena-role-private-sector.

Lomas, Natasha. "Uber Is Paying $3.1BN to Pick Up Middle East Rival Careem." *TechCrunch,* March 26, 2019. https://techcrunch.com/2019/03/26/uber-is-paying-3-1bn-to-pick-up-middle-east-rival-careem.

Making Waves. "Ep 9 - Mudassir Sheikha, Careem." August 30, 2016. Video, 4:36. https://www.youtube.com/watch?v=4Z6w9Wlxvrs.

Mitchell, Alex. "Top 10 Middle East Startups to Watch in 2020." *Medium,* February 18, 2020. https://blog.usejournal.com/top-10-middle-east-startups-to-watch-in-2020-d2126096bb6b.

Momentum Tech Conference. "Mudassir Sheikha Speech." June 11, 2017. Video, 25:03. https://www.youtube.com/watch?v=hbcUYGj-U68.

Mottaghi, Lili. "Invest in Women to Boost Growth in MENA." *World Bank Blogs,* March 6, 2019. https://blogs.worldbank.org/arabvoices/invest-women-boost-growth-mena.

OPEN Silicon Valley. "Founder Series - Careem Co-Founder and CEO Mudassir Sheikha." April 21, 2019. Video, 7:23. https://www.youtube.com/watch?v=3S9Bi8DQy34.

Rakuten Group Official. "Interview with Mudassir Sheikha at NEST 2017." June 1, 2017. Video, 4:21. https://www.youtube.com/watch?v=U-vPNGa-RLq8.

Rizwan, Asra. "Almost 300 Careem Employees Will Become Millionaires as a Result of Uber Acquisition." *Techjuice,* March 27, 2021. https://www.techjuice.pk/almost-300-careem-employees-will-become-millionaires-as-a-result-of-uber-acquisition/.

Schwartz, Tony and Christine Porath. "Why You Hate Work." *The New York Times,* May 30, 2014. https://www.nytimes.com/2014/06/01/opinion/sunday/why-you-hate-work.html.

Specia, Megan. "Saudi Arabia Granted Women the Right to Drive. A Year on, It's Still Complicated." *The New York Times,* June 24, 2019. https://www.nytimes.com/2019/06/24/world/middleeast/saudi-driving-ban-anniversary.html.

Talks at Google. "Careem Co-Founders | Mudassir Sheikha & Magnus Olsson | Talks at Google." December 11, 2017. Video, 47:17. https://www.youtube.com/watch?v=ek3qkUuE_hU.

The DMZ. "Mudassir Sheikha Talks RiDe-hailing App Careem with Abdullah Snobar." October 21, 2019. Video, 1:13:19. https://www.youtube.com/watch?v=E-tOVjtdo8M.

The Nest I/O. "021Disrupt 2019 | The Careem Story by Mudassir Sheikha." December 2, 2019. Video, 45:25. https://www.youtube.com/watch?v=g9up87QMOY4.

"Unveiling the 2020 Zeno Strength of Purpose Study." *Zeno.* June 17, 2020. https://www.zenogroup.com/insights/2020-zeno-strength-purpose.

Woetzel, Jonathan, Anu Madgavkar, Kweilin Ellingrud, Eric Labaye, Sandrine Devillard, Eric Kutcher, James Manyika, Richard Dobbs, and Mekala Krishnan. "How Advancing Women's Equality Can Add $12 Trillion to Global Growth." *McKinsey Global Institute,* September 1, 2015. https://www.mckinsey.com/featured-insights/employment-

and-growth/how-advancing-womens-equality-can-add-12-trillion-to-global-growth.

World101. "Middle East & North Africa Explained | World101." February 27, 2020. Video, 8:34. https://www.youtube.com/watch?v=-YUI2t-8FNvE.

CHAPTER 5: QUEEN OF REFRAMING

APEC Summit. "Success story of A Taiwanese Entrepreneur." March 27, 2012. Video, 38:09. https://www.youtube.com/watch?v=EhyvS2Z1b9c.

"Cher Wang: Journey to Success," *IIT Delhi.* Accessed December 29, 2020. https://ecelliitd.wordpress.com/2020/06/14/journey-to-success-cher-wang/.

Computer Hope. "Computer History - 1983." Accessed December 28, 2020. https://www.computerhope.com/history/1983.htm.

First International Computer, Inc. "First International Computer, Inc. - Company Profile, Information, Business Description, History, Background Information on First International Computer, Inc." Accessed December 28, 2020. https://www.referenceforbusiness.com/history2/40/First-International-Computer-Inc.html.

Haden, Jeff. "A Study of 2.7 Million Startups Found the Ideal Age to Start a Business (and It's Much Older Than You Think)." *Inc,* July 16, 2018. https://www.inc.com/jeff-haden/a-study-of-27-million-startups-found-ideal-age-to-start-a-business-and-its-much-older-than-you-think.html.

Holson, Laura. "With Smartphones, Cher Wang Made Her Own Fortune." *The New York Times,* October 26, 2008. https://www.nytimes.com/2008/10/27/technology/companies/27wang.html.

Rappler. "Cher Wang at the APEC SME Summit." January 22, 2013. Video, 11:57. https://www.youtube.com/watch?v=2CXnjDgKA1M.

Savitz, Eric. "Cher Wang: The Most Powerful Woman in Wireless." *Forbes,* October 26, 2011. https://www.forbes.com/sites/ericsavitz/2011/10/26/cher-wang-the-most-powerful-woman-in-wireless-takes-on-apple.

Swingle, Joshua. "HTC Just Experienced Revenue Growth for the First Time This Year." *PhoneArea,* December 9, 2020. https://www.phonearena.com/news/htc-november-2020-revenue-growth_id128804#.

Taylor, Chris. "70% of Rich Families Lose Their Wealth by the Second Generation." June 17, 2015. https://money.com/rich-families-lose-wealth/.

The Associated Press. "Y. C. Wang, Billionaire Who Led Formosa Plastics, Is Dead at 91." *The New York Times,* October 16, 2008. https://www.nytimes.com/2008/10/17/business/17wang.html.

"Top Hot 100 singles of 1974," *Billboard Magazine.*

"Women in Business: Why Taiwan Is a Supportive Space for Entrepreneurs." *Standard Chartered,* November 21, 2019. https://www.sc.com/en/feature/women-entrepreneurs-taiwan.

CHAPTER 6: IT TAKES A VILLAGE

Aboyeji, Iyinoluwa. "How Andela was founded...." *Medium,* June 19, 2016. https://medium.com/@iaboyeji/how-andela-was-founded-f32b22808b8a.

Amazon Web Services. "Hiring Top Talent for Your Startup (Lessons from Andela)." March 28, 2019. Video, 53:07. https://www.youtube.com/watch?v=LWF_uaT4TC8.

Anderson, Stuart. "Low Unemployment Rate in Tech Harms Trump H-1B Visa Plans." *Forbes,* May 18, 2020. https://www.forbes.com/sites/stuartanderson/2020/05/18/low-unemployment-rate-in-tech-harms-trump-h-1b-visa-plans.

Arguden, Yilmaz. "Why Boards Need More Women." *Harvard Business Review*, June 7, 2012. https://hbr.org/2012/06/why-boards-need-more-women

Arise News. "Nadayar Enegesi, Co-Founder of Andela Discusses the Tech Ecosystem in Nigeria." May 3, 2018. Video, 12:41. https://www.youtube.com/watch?v=5YEs16KeM9I.

Awomodu, Gbenga. "Nigeria's Got Hope! – Meet Iyinoluwa Aboyeji, 19-Year-Old Co-founder of Promising Online Startup, Bookneto." *Bella Naija*, January 27, 2011. https://www.bellanaija.com/2011/01/nigerias-got-hope-meet-iyinoluwa-aboyeji-19-year-old-co-founder-of-promising-online-startup-bookneto/.

Benson, Emmanuel Abara. "Africa's Startup Ecosystem Now Has 4 Unicorns Valued at over $1 Billion Each." *Business Elites Africa,* March 15, 2021. https://businesselitesafrica.com/2021/03/15/african-unicorn-startups/.

Biztorials TV. "Who's Idea Was Andela?" June 17, 2016. Video, 4:25. https://www.youtube.com/watch?v=iVZoYxOEuvQ.

Bloomberg Technology. "How Andela Discovers Africa's Untapped Tech Talent." October 4, 2016. Video, 3:59. https://www.youtube.com/watch?v=RMuK2Hby3Eg.

Bright, Jake. "What Is Andela, The Africa Tech Talent Accelerator," "#Siliconvalleysowhite: Black Facebook and Google Employees Speak Out on Big Tech Racism." *TechCrunch,* August 29, 2019. https://techcrunch.com/2019/08/29/what-is-andela-the-africa-tech-talent-accelerator/.

CNBCAfrica. "EA Debate: Start-up Funding - Lessons from the Andela Story." August 21, 2018. Video, 28:18. https://www.youtube.com/watch?v=zeMUviSqw_E.

Feldman, Amy. "Andela: Next Billion-Dollar Startups." *Forbes*, May 27, 2020. https://www.forbes.com/sites/amyfeldman/2020/05/28/next-billion-dollar-startups-2020/.

Finley, Klint. "This Company Is Paying Nigerians to Learn Computer Programming." *Wired*, December 18, 2014. https://www.wired.com/2014/12/andela.

"Flutterwave Raises $170M at over $1 Billion Valuation." *Brandcrunch*, March 10, 2021. https://www.brandcrunch.com.ng/2021/03/10/flutterwave-raises-170m-at-over-1-billion-valuation/.

Guynn, Jessica. "#Siliconvalleysowhite: Black Facebook and Google Employees Speak Out on Big Tech Racism." *USA Today.* February 10, 2020. https://www.usatoday.com/story/tech/2020/02/10/racial-discrimination-persists-facebook-google-employees-say/4307591002/.

Iyinoluwa Aboyeji. "Flutterwave Pitch." August 11, 2016. Video, 3:07. https://www.youtube.com/watch?v=DNETfs7w5-o.

Joy, Lois, Harvey Wagner, and Siriam Narayanan. "Report: The Bottom Line: Corporate Performance and Women's Representation on Boards." *Catalyst,* October 15, 2007. https://www.catalyst.org/research/the-bottom-line-corporate-performance-and-womens-representation-on-boards/.

Kaestner, Henry and William Norvell. "Episode 55 - The Continent of Potential with Iyinoluwa Aboyeji." March 14, 2021. In *Faith Driven Investor.* Produced by Henry Kaestner. Podcast, MP3 audio, 18:46. http://www.npr.org/podcasts/510303/how-to-do-everything.

Kazeem, Yomi. "Andela's Latest $100 Million Funding Round Is Led by a Former US Vice President." *Quartz Africa*, January 23, 2019. https://qz.com/africa/1531075/andela-raises-100-million-series-d-round-from-al-gore-led-vc/.

Kene-Okafor, Tage. "Andela Begins Global Expansion in 37 Countries Months after Going Remote across Africa." *TechCrunch,* April

18, 2021. https://autos.yahoo.com/andela-begins-global-expansion-37-075709662.html.

Kene-Okafor, Tage. "How African Startups Raised Investments in 2020." *TechCrunch,* February 11, 2021. https://techcrunch.com/2021/02/11/how-african-startups-raised-investments-in-2020/.

Kimani, Michael. "African Startups Should Tokenize to Break Biased Funding Cycles." *Coindesk,* November 11, 2020. https://www.coindesk.com/african-startups-should-tokenize-to-break-biased-funding-cycles.

Matranga, Heather. "Why Do Investors Continue to Shortchange Entrepreneurs in Emerging Markets?" *Village Capital Medium,* May 11, 2017. https://medium.com/village-capital/why-do-investors-continue-to-shortchange-entrepreneurs-in-emerging-markets-f57a8b-f4a7d8.

"Nigeria Plane Crash Kills 107, Mostly Children." *The New York Times,* December 11, 2005. https://www.nytimes.com/2005/12/11/world/africa/nigeria-plane-crash-kills-107-mostly-children.html.

Njoki, Adeliade and Stephen Gugu. "Bridging the Gap Between Local and Expat Founder Funding." *Viktoria Ventures,* April 10, 2020. http://viktoria.co.ke/blog/bridging-the-gap-between-local-and-expat-founder-funding/.

Our Eden Life. "Home." Accessed April 2021. https://ouredenlife.com/.

Pang, Kelly. "The New Silk Road - The Belt and Road Initiative." *China Highlights*, April 25, 2021. https://www.chinahighlights.com/silkroad/new-silk-road.htm#.

Pulkkinen, Levi. "If Silicon Valley Were a Country, It Would Be Among the Richest on Earth." *The Guardian*, April 30, 2019. https://www.theguardian.com/technology/2019/apr/30/silicon-valley-wealth-second-richest-country-world-earth.

Roberts, Ian. Interview with Michael Bervell. May 2021.

Spero Ventures. "Jeremy Johnson, Cofounder and CEO of Andela." August 21, 2017. Video, 22:38. https://www.youtube.com/watch?v=z-osO2-Twu9k.

Statista, "Distributed Workforce among Enterprises Worldwide before and after the COVID-19 Pandemic in 2020." Last modified January 11, 2021. Accessed April 2021. https://www.statista.com/statistics/1184602/distributed-workplace-enterprises-coronavirus/.

Teare, Gené. "Global Venture Funding Hits All-Time Record High $125B In Q1 2021." *Crunchbase News,* April 7, 2021. https://news.crunchbase.com/news/global-venture-hits-an-all-time-high-in-q1-2021-a-record-125-billion-funding/

TechCrunch. "Andela's Christina Sass on Growing Tech Talent in Africa at Disrupt SF." September 14, 2016. Video, 20:35. https://www.youtube.com/watch?v=LGbYlfSOozI.

TEDx Talks. "The Return on Diversity | Jeremy Johnson | TEDxCornellTech." June 2, 2016. Video, 15:09. https://www.youtube.com/watch?v=f6tv7BhtdY8.

TEDx Talks. "When Will Africa's Elite Grow Up? | Iyinoluwa Aboyeji | TEDxEuston" February 8, 2019. Video, 14:25. https://www.youtube.com/watch?v=Fxua94bRJPo.

The Foursquare Church. "About." Accessed April 2021. https://www.foursquare.org/about/.

"The Pandemic Is Hurting China's Belt and Road Initiative." *The Economist,* June 4, 2020. https://www.economist.com/china/2020/06/04/the-pandemic-is-hurting-chinas-belt-and-road-initiative.

"The Software Developer Shortage in the US and the Global Tech Talent Shortage in 2021." *Daxx,* November 13, 2020. https://www.daxx.com/blog/development-trends/software-developer-shortage-us.

This Week in Startups. "E862 Andela Jeremy Johnson: Trains Africa's Software Engineers, Connecting Growing Pop. & Global Need." October 5, 2018. Video, 1:03:08. https://www.youtube.com/watch?v=n-jiQ1QBotqo.

VC Videos. "VCFinTech Demo Day - Flutterwave." August 11, 2016. Video, 12:38. https://www.youtube.com/watch?v=WYUE0ZSjKA4

CHAPTER 7: PIVOT PLAYER

"Baidu - Company Overview." Accessed November 30, 2020. https://ir.baidu.com/company-overview.

Bajwa Sohaib S., Xiaofen Wang, Anh Duc Nguyen, and Pekka Abrahamsson. "Failures to Be Celebrated: An Analysis of Major Pivots of Software Startups." *Empir Software Eng* 22: 2373 (2017). https://arxiv.org/pdf/1710.04037.pdf.

Barboza, David. "The Rise of Baidu (That's Chinese for Google)." *New York Times,* September 17, 2006. https://www.nytimes.com/2006/09/17/business/yourmoney/17baidu.html.

"Everyone Pivots: The Truth About a Startup Pivot." *The Startups Team,* October 31, 2017. https://www.startups.com/library/expert-advice/startup-business-pivot.

Hendy, Carl. "1995 - The Dawn of Search Engines." Accessed November 30, 2020. https://carlhendy.com/history-of-search-engines/#robinli.

Lin, Qiu. "Searching for Success: Robin Li." *China Daily,* October 7, 2009. http://www.chinadaily.com.cn/bizchina///2009-10/07/content_8766368.htm.

NY Times News Service. "Robin Li's Vision Powers Baidu's Internet Search Dominance." *Taipei Times,* September 17, 2006. http://www.taipeitimes.com/News/bizfocus/archives/2006/09/17/2003328060.

Page, Lawrence. 1997. Method for Node Ranking in a Linked Database. US. US6285999B1, January 10, 1997, Issued September 4, 2001. https://patents.google.com/patent/US6285999B1/en.

"Rankdex: The Qualitative Web Search Engine." Accessed November 29, 2020. http://www.rankdex.com/index.html.

"Robin Li the Founder of Baidu." *Luxatic.* Accessed November 30, 2020. https://luxatic.com/robin-li-the-founder-of-baidu/.

Smith, Craig. "Baidu Statistics and Facts (2021). | By the Numbers." *DMR,* March 23, 2021. https://expandedramblings.com/index.php/baidu-stats/.

Stanford Technology Ventures Program. "Lessons From China: The Evolution of the Globe's Largest Search Engine." September 23, 2009. In *Entrepreneurial Thought Leaders.* Produced by DFJ Entrepreneurial Thought Leader Series. Podcast, MP3 audio, 52:47. https://ecorner.stanford.edu/podcasts/lessons-from-china-the-evolution-of-the-globes-largest-search-engine/

Vashishtha, Yashica. "Robin Li: The Founder of Baidu, the 'Google of China.'" *Your Tech Story,* August 25, 2019. https://www.yourtechstory.com/2019/08/25/robin-li-founder-baidu-google-china/.

Viva Technology. "Robin Li, Founder, Chairman and CEO of Baidu | Interview | VivaTech." July 13, 2016. Video, 34:06. https://www.youtube.com/watch?v=cNP1-vMbvuw.

"Xin Qiji - Famous Words." Accessed November 30, 2020. https://mingyanjiaju.org/lang-en/mr/7098.html.

CHAPTER 8: STRATEGIC AMBITIONS

BML Munjal University. "Ritesh Agarwal Inspiring BMU Students on Convocation." January 31, 2019. Video, 24:20. https://www.youtube.com/watch?v=GJHPwxVECBc.

CNBC-TV18. "OYO Founder Ritesh Agarwal Tells His Story at Young Turks Conclave 2018." November 3, 2018. Video, 23:26. https://www.youtube.com/watch?v=liV6iTZif-4.

Daniel, Anand. "INSIGHTS#34 Ritesh Agarwal on building OYO – Decacorn in the Hotel Industry." July 26, 2019. In *SEED TO SCALE Podcast Series by Accel.* Produced by Accel Ventures. Podcast, MP3 audio, 34:30. https://www.seedtoscale.com/content/building-oyo-decacorn-in-the-hotel-industry.

Ghosh, Shona. "The founder of SoftBank-backed Hotel Startup Oyo is Buying Back Shares in His Company in a $1.5 Billion Deal." *Business Insider,* October 7, 2019. https://www.businessinsider.com/oyo-raises-15-billion-from-ceo-and-other-backers-at-10-billion-valuation-2019-10.

Gupta, Abhishek. "Annual Report Card FY 2019." *Official OYO Blog,* February 17, 2020. https://www.oyorooms.com/officialoyoblog/2020/02/17/annual-report-card-fy-2019.

Hansen, Drew. "Why Marriott's Days as the World's Largest Hotelier Could End Early Next Year." *Washington Business Journal,* December 6, 2019. https://www.bizjournals.com/washington/news/2019/12/06/why-marriotts-days-as-the-worlds-largest-hotelier.html.

How to Start a Startup IIM Ahmedabad. "How to Start a Startup | Session 5 - Ritesh Agarwal." February 25, 2017. Video, 30:00. https://www.youtube.com/watch?v=snychWgbJxU.

Khatri, Bhumika. "OYO Receives Shock from the Past Amid Mounting Troubles." *Inc42,* January 28, 2020. https://inc42.com/buzz/oyo-vs-zo-rooms-oyo-gets-shock-from-the-past-amid-mounting-troubles.

Mishra, Anhish. "Will the Real Ritesh Agarwal Please Stand Up?" *Mint,* January 7, 2015. https://www.livemint.com/Companies/7CN7u5d4i3b-fYgBAZLdLpM/Will-the-real-Ritesh-Agarwal-please-stand-up.html.

"OYO Founder, Ritesh Agarwal, Named the Youngest Indian Billionaire by Hurun." *The Economic Times,* February 29, 2020. https://economic-times.indiatimes.com/small-biz/startups/newsbuzz/oyo-founder-ritesh-agarwal-named-the-youngest-indian-billionaire-by-hurun/articleshow/74333773.cms.

Phocuswright. "Keynote: OYO Hotels & Homes - The Phocuswright Conference." November 20, 2019. Video, 27:39. https://www.youtube.com/watch?v=9zFc-o5UpEU.

The Journey Guide. "Youngest Billionaire of World| OYO Rooms | Ritesh Agarwal | Inspirational | Nas Daily." March 10, 2020. Video, 3:58. https://www.youtube.com/watch?v=caQolZNJc3Y.

VCC TV. "Ritesh Agarwal, Founder & CEO, OYO Rooms." August 25, 2015. Video, 17:07. https://www.youtube.com/watch?v=y2Lk8TExz6w.

Venkat. "OYO Rooms: You Stay in Hotel 'On Your Own' Terms." Harvard Business School, February 28, 2017. https://digital.hbs.edu/platform-digit/submission/oyo-rooms-you-stay-in-hotel-on-your-own-terms/.

YourStory. "Ep 14: Unfiltered with Ritesh Agarwal: All Things Money & Growth | Money Matters with Shradha Sharma." May 25, 2020. Video, 1:10:38. https://www.youtube.com/watch?v=Z-SQN9hea60.

CHAPTER 9: THE PARTNERSHIP DECACORN

"Banking Southeast Asia's Unbanked." *The Asean Post*, January 1, 2019. https://theaseanpost.com/article/banking-southeast-asias-un-banked-0.

Bloomberg Technology. "Grab Co-Founders Anthony Tan and Hooi Ling Tan on 'Bloomberg Studio 1.0.'" August 15, 2019. Video, 24:04. https://www.youtube.com/watch?v=kMq5mF7dry0.

Chrzanowska, Natalia. "Global Success Achieved Locally – Uber Ice Cream Campaign." *Brand24*, September 15, 2015. https://brand24.com/blog/global-success-locally-uber-ice-cream-campaign/.

"Economic Outlook for Southeast Asia, China and India 2020: Rethinking Education for the Digital Era." *Organisation for Economic Co-operation and Development*, OECD, 2019. https://www.oecd.org/dev/asia-pacific/SAEO2020_PRELIMINARY_VERSION_FOR_WEB.pdf.

Goldman Sachs. "Hooi Ling Tan: Co-Founder of Grab." May 22, 2019. Video, 21:57. https://www.youtube.com/watch?v=8wpSLqVj318.

"Languages in Southeast Asia." April 12, 2018. Accessed January 2021. https://bilingua.io/languages-in-southeast-asia-complete-guide.

Lee, Yoolim, Tom Giles, and Haslinda Amin. "Ride-Hailing Giant Grab Expects to Double Revenue in 2019." *Bloomberg*, September 5, 2018. https://www.bloomberg.com/news/articles/2018-09-06/ride-hailing-giant-grab-expects-to-double-revenue-in-2019.

McCall, Olivia. "Woman to Watch: Grab Co-Founder Hooi Ling Tan." *Born2Invest*, September 30, 2017. https://born2invest.com/articles/grab-co-founder-hooi-ling-tan/.

Morris, Cheryl. "2011 Harvard Business Plan Contest: Winners Awarded After 9 Phenomenal Finalist Pitches." *Boston: American Inno*, April 26, 2011. https://www.americaninno.com/boston/2011-harvard-business-plan-contest-winners-announced-after-9-finalist-pitches/.

Nikkei Asia. "Tan Hooi Ling, Co-founder (Grab): How Technology Changes Society." November 2019. Video, 31:41. https://www.youtube.com/watch?v=RoYqtkW_srU.

"Religions of Southeast Asia." Accessed January 2021. https://southasiaoutreach.wisc.edu/religions/.

RISE Conference. "In Conversation with Grab." July 11, 2018. Video, 25:10. https://www.youtube.com/watch?v=FpfmlMkQxFM.

RISE Conference. "Staying Ahead in the Real Time Taxi Wars - Tan Hooi Ling & David Rowan." June 9, 2016. Video, 27:55. https://www.youtube.com/watch?v=Ei8xIRPhj6I.

Russell, Jon. "Grab's Acquisition of Uber Southeast Asia Drives into Problems." *TechCrunch*, April 24, 2018. https://techcrunch.com/2018/04/24/grab-uber-deal-southeast-asia/.

Russell, Jon. "GrabTaxi Raises $65 Million to Increase the Competition with Uber in Southeast Asia." *TechCrunch*, October 20, 2014. https://techcrunch.com/2014/10/20/grabtaxi-raises-65-million-to-increase-the-competition-with-uber-in-southeast-asia/.

Russell, Jon. "Uber and Grab Hit With $9.5m in Fines over 'Anti-competitive' Merger." *TechCrunch,* September 23, 2018. https://techcrunch.com/2018/09/23/uber-and-grab-hit-with-9-5m-in-fines/.

Scott, Mary. "GrabTaxi's 'Other' Founder Talks About Return to Company." *Forbes Asia,* November 17, 2015. https://www.forbes.com/sites/forbesasia/2015/11/17/grabtaxis-other-founder-talks-about-return-to-company.

Sen, Antarika. "Who Are the Investors behind Grab?" *The Low Down Momentum Asia,* January 31, 2019. https://thelowdown.momentum.asia/who-are-the-investors-behind-grab/.

"Southeast Asian Countries." Accessed January 2021. https://www.niu.edu/clas/cseas/resources/countries.shtml.

"South-Eastern Asia Population." Accessed January 2021. https://www.worldometers.info/world-population/south-eastern-asia-population/.

Suzuki, Yusuke. "Megacities in Southeast Asia - The Progression of Unipolar Concentration and Expansion into the Suburbs." *Mitsui & Co. Global Strategic Studies Institute (MGSSI),* March 2019: 1-7. https://www.mitsui.com/mgssi/en/report/detail/__icsFiles/afieldfile/2019/05/07/1903d_suzuki.pdf_e.pdf.

Tan, Sumiko. "Lunch With Sumiko: Grab Whiz Tan Hooi Ling Happy to Stay Low-key." *The Straits Times,* July 16, 2017. https://www.straitstimes.com/singapore/grab-whiz-happy-to-stay-low-key.

Teng, Liew J. "Newsmakers 2017: The Tans behind Southeast Asia's Highest Value Tech Start-Up." *The Edge Markets*, January 5, 2018. https://www.theedgemarkets.com/article/newsmakers-2017-tans-behind-southeast-asias-highest-value-tech-startup.

The New York Times. "Durian - The World's Smelliest Fruit | The New York Times." December 5, 2013. Video, 2:20. https://www.youtube.com/watch?v=U4p4K7sPPLM.

"Toyota Pumps $1 Billion in Grab in Auto Industry's Biggest Ride-hailing Bet." *Reuters*, June 12, 2018. https://www.reuters.com/article/us-grab-toyota-investment/toyota-pumps-1-billion-in-grab-in-auto-industrys-biggest-ride-hailing-bet-idUSKBN1J907E.

CHAPTER 10: CONTENT-MARKET FIT

"방시혁 "가수 자질?...무대 지배하는 사람." *SBS News,* April 11, 2011. https://news.sbs.co.kr/news/endPage.do?news_id=N1000893945.

중앙일보. "2010 '히트곡 메이커' <1> 방시혁." *Joins News*, March 30, 2010. https://news.joins.com/article/4085543.

"10 Mind-Blowing BTS Facts and Statistics." *Brandwatch*, January 20, 2021. https://www.brandwatch.com/blog/bts-facts-and-statistics/.

Asian Entertainment and Culture. "Details of The Harvard Business School Paper about BTS and Big Hit: BTS Success & Challenges." July 12, 2020. Video, 20:10. https://www.youtube.com/watch?v=aYX-bUy31OIk.

BangtanSubs. "(ENG) 180223 Good Insight Season 2." 2019. Video, 52:59. https://www.dailymotion.com/video/x6y2b23.

Berima Amo TV. "Berima Amo - Yaa Amponsah (Best Rendition)." January 5, 2019. Video, 1:29. https://www.youtube.com/watch?v=GWdhL_Pmzy4.

Brown, Harley. "BTS' Agency Big Hit Entertainment Valued Over $1B, According to Think Tank." *Billboard,* June 6, 2019. https://www.billboard.com/articles/business/8514793/bts-agency-big-hit-entertainment-valued-over-1-billion.

Bruner, Raisa. "The Mastermind Behind BTS Opens Up About Making a K-Pop Juggernaut." *Time,* October 8, 2019. https://time.com/5681494/bts-bang-si-hyuk-interview/.

Collins, John, "An Interview with John Collins on Cultural Policy, Folklore and the Recording Industry in Ghana." *The World of Music*, Vol. 36, No. 2, The Guitar in Africa: The 1950s – 1990s (1994). https://www.jstor.org/stable/43561391?seq=1.

Dzurillay, Julia. "BTS by the Numbers: Is This K-Pop Group Really Bigger Than the Beatles?" *Showbiz CheatSheet,* January 20, 2020. https://www.cheatsheet.com/entertainment/bts-k-pop-group-the-beatles.html/.

Elegant, Naomi. "BTS Members' Net Worth Balloons by Millions as Their Music Label Stages a Massive IPO." *Fortune,* October 15, 2020. https://fortune.com/2020/10/15/bts-net-worth-big-hit-ipo/.

Gollayan, Christian. "K-Pop Band BTS Brings $3.6 Billion a Year to South Korea." *New York Post,* December 18, 2018. https://nypost.com/2018/12/18/k-pop-band-bts-brings-3-6-billion-a-year-to-south-korea/.

"Global Music-Streaming: 'for Growth You Have to Look Outside of the Western Markets.'" *Musically,* January 22, 2019. https://musically.com/2019/01/22/global-music-streaming-for-growth-you-have-to-look-outside-of-the-western-markets/.

Herman, Tamar. "Digitally-Savvy and Passionate, K-Pop Fans' Trump Activism Should Come As No Surprise." *The Guardian*, June 22, 2020. https://www.theguardian.com/commentisfree/2020/jun/22/digitally-savvy-and-passionate-k-pop-fans-trump-activism-should-come-as-no-surprise.

Ingham, Tim. "English-language Music is Losing its Stranglehold on Global Pop Charts — and YouTube is Driving the Change." *Music Business Worldwide*, February 3, 2019. https://www.musicbusinessworldwide.com/english-language-music-is-losing-its-stranglehold-on-global-pop-charts-and-youtube-proves-it/.

Ji-hyoung, Son. "Bang Si-Hyuk: From 'Hitman' to 'Motivator.'" *K-Pop Herald,* March 3, 2017. http://kpopherald.koreaherald.com/view.php?ud=201703032117427077167_2.

Joonie Toon. "A Guide to the BTS Staff: Bang PD." March 29, 2018. Video, 9:43. https://www.youtube.com/watch?v=QRzLyITvyqE.

Katsiaficas, George. *Asia's Unknown Uprisings Volume 1: South Korean Social Movements in the 20th Century.* Oakland: PM Press, 2012.

Kelley, Caitlin. "K-Pop Is More Global Than Ever, Helping South Korea's Music Market Grow Into a 'Power Player.'" *Forbes,* April 3, 2019. https://www.forbes.com/sites/caitlinkelley/2019/04/03/kpop-global-bts-blackpink-grow/.

Kim, Sohee. "The $4.7 Billion K-Pop Industry Chases Its 'Michael Jackson Moment.'" *Bloomberg Businessweek,* August 22, 2017. https://www.bloomberg.com/news/articles/2017-08-22/the-4-7-billion-k-pop-industry-chases-its-michael-jackson-moment.

KOREA NOW. "(FULL VER.) BTS Hitman Bang Si-Hyuk's Speech on Good Content at Asean-Rok Culture Innovation Summit." November 26, 2019. Video, 10:46. https://www.youtube.com/watch?v=U66rRd-3PgG8.

MBCfestival. "Taijiboys - I know, 서태지와 아이들 - 난 알아요, Saturday Night Music Show 19920815." December 12, 2012. Video, 5:26. https://www.youtube.com/watch?v=JKK0UEu4Q5g.

Romano, Aja. "How K-Pop Became a Global Phenomenon." *Vox*, February 26, 2018. https://www.vox.com/culture/2018/2/16/16915672/what-is-kpop-history-explained.

"Seoul National University Rankings." Accessed February 2021. https://edurank.org/uni/seoul-national-university/.

Sherylle, Jeniffer. "BANG SI HYUK Reveals How He Chose BTS's Members, Why He Made an Idol Group – KpopHit I BTS'(방탄소년단)." April 16, 2020. Video, 3:31. https://www.youtube.com/watch?v=-JQ5rNRsoVS4.

Statista, "Highest Grossing Film Franchises and Series 2020." Last modified January 13, 2021. Accessed February 2021. https://www.statista.com/statistics/317408/highest-grossing-film-franchises-series/.

Statista, "K-Pop Popularity Worldwide 2020." Last modified February 2, 2021. Accessed February 2021. https://www.statista.com/statistics/937232/south-korea-kpop-popularity-worldwide.

The ARMY vlog. "The Secret to BTS's Success | Arirang World - 4angles." July 19, 2017. Video, 5:23. https://www.youtube.com/watch?v=cjMQ-jPJPQjk.

"The BTS Billions: K-Pop Superstars 'Worth More Than US$3.6 Billion a Year' to South Korea's Economy." *South China Morning Post,* December 18, 2018. https://www.scmp.com/news/asia/east-asia/article/2178540/bts-billions-k-pop-superstars-worth-more-us36-billion-year-south.

Vanity Fair. "BTS Breaks Down Their Music Career | Vanity Fair." December 17, 2020. Video, 10:59. https://www.youtube.com/watch?v=-r9jEW-sQkXs.

Waitt, Hannah. "The History of K-Pop, Chapter 1: The Politics of K-Pop."
   MoonROK, June 16, 2014. http://www.moonrok.com/tag/the-history-of-k-pop-10/.

Weatherby, Taylor. "Psy's 'Gangnam Style' Has Officially Lost the Title of
   Most-Watched YouTube Video." *Billboard,* July 11, 2018. https://www.
   billboard.com/articles/columns/pop/7864953/psy-gangnam-style-
   video-most-watched-youtube-record-see-you-again.

CONCLUSION

Clark, Ralph. "More Equity: Ralph Clark, a CEO Connoisseur." Interview
   with Michael Bervell. *Harlem Capital More Equity Podcast,* Podcast
   Audio, October 2020. https://open.spotify.com/episode/0YoLA7BX-
   vYXnB2s35hBwgP.

Wahba, Phil. "Only 19: The Lack of Black CEOs in the History of the Fortune 500." *Fortune,* February 1, 2021. https://fortune.com/longform/
   fortune-500-black-ceos-business-history/.

ENDNOTES

———

1 Bervell 2020

2 Alspach 2012

3 McKinsey 2019

4 Business Insider 2019

5 Campbell 2019

6 Statista 2021

7 Crocodile 2015

8 Stanford 2011

9 CNBC Africa 2018

10 CNBC Africa 2018

11 Stanford 2011

12 Reynolds, 2017

13 Gage 2012

14 Stanford 2015

15 Crocodile 2015

16 NTV Kenya 2017

17 NTV Kenya 2017

18 NTV Kenya 2017

19 NTV Kenya 2017

20 Wenderoth 2018

21 Belli 2017

22 Farnam 2011

23 Crocodile 2015

24 CNBC 2017

25 Stanford 2015

26 Stanford 2015

27 Stanford 2015

28 Crocodile 2015

29 Stanford 2015

30 Moscow State 2019

31 January 2021

32 Forbes, 2020

33 Time 2010; Financial Times 2020

34 Science History Institute 2013

35 Dr. Kiran Mazumdar Shaw 2020

36 Science History Institute 2013

37 Science History Institute,
    2013

38 ENDEVR, 2020

39 Science History Institute
    2013

40 World Bank Group, 2020

41 The Wire 2016

42 Myers 2010

43 Sadhguru 2017

44 Sadhguru 2017

45 Sadhguru 2017

46 Science History Institute
    2013

47 BBC News 2018

48 ENDEVR 2020

49 ENDEVR 2020

50 Science History Institute
    2013

51 Business Wire 2017

52 Score 2020

53 Crunchbase 2020

54 Science History Institute
    2013

55 BBC News 2018

56 ENDEVR 2020

57 ENDEVR 2020

58 Science History Institute
    2013

59 Science History Institute
    2013

60 Science History Institute
    2013

61 BBC 2018

62 PR Newswire 2019

63 Business Insider 2017

64 Science History Institute
    2013

65 BBC News 2018

66 BBC News 2018

67 Science History Institute
    2013

68 ENDEVR 2020

69 PR Newswire 2019

70 ENDEVR 2020

71 ENDEVR 2020

72 Her Power 2015

73 The Economic Times 2020

74 Her Power 2015

75 WeeTracker, 2019 /Techca-
    bal, 2020

76 Quartz Africa, 2020

77 Affinity, 2021

78 World Bank, 2021

79 Statista, 2014

80 Statista, 2021

81 Statista, 2021

82 Statista, 2021

83 Economist Books, 2019

84 TechCrunch, 2019

85 InterswitchSPAK, 2020

86 TEDx, 2012

87 TEDx ,2012

88 SPICE Nigeria, 2008

89 SPICE Nigeria, 2008

90 Technology Times, 2020

91 Spice Nigeria, 2008

92 Nigerian Informer, 2019

93 Bridge Leadership Foundation, 2020

94 Bridge Leadership Foundation, 2020

95 Bridge Leadership Foundation, 2020

96 Bridge Leadership Foundation, 2020

97 Bridge Leadership Foundation, 2020

98 Bridge Leadership Foundation, 2020

99 The Banker, 2013

100 Bridge Leadership Foundation, 2020

101 Lagos Business School, 2019

102 Fortumo, 2015

103 Biz Watch Nigeria 2019

104 Statista 2020

105 Visa 2019

106 Bridge Leadership Foundation 2020

107 Bridge Leadership Foundation 2020

108 TechCrunch 2020

109 TC Video 2020

110 Bridge Leadership Foundation 2020

111 World Economic Forum 2020

112 TC Video 2020

113 LABS 2020

114 World101 2020

115 Medium, 2020 / TechCrunch 2019

116 Investopedia 2021

117 International Monetary Fund 2012

118 World Bank Blogs 2019; Business Chief 2020; McKinsey Global Institute 2015

119 FastCompany 2021

120 Careem 2021

121 Momentum Tech Conference 2017

122 OPEN Silicon Valley 2019

123 OPEN Silicon Valley 2019

124 The Nest I/O 2019

125 OPEN Silicon Valley 2019

126 Making Waves 2016

127 Endeavour Jordan 2016

128 Making Waves 2016

129 Endeavour Jordan 2016

130 Talks at Google 2017

131 Talks at Google 2017

132 Talks at Google 2017

133 Endeavour Jordan 2016

134 The Nest I/O 2019

135 Endeavour Jordan 2016

136   Talks at Google 2017

137   Talks at Google 2017

138   Rise Conference 2018

139   Rise Conference 2018

140   Zeno 2020

141   The New York Times 2014

142   Rise Conference 2018

143   Endeavor Jordan 2016

144   Endeavor Jordan 2016

145   Rakuten Group 2017

146   Endeavor Jordan 2016

147   Endeavor Jordan 2016

148   Talks at Google 2017

149   Endeavor Jordan 2016

150   GXTalks 2019

151   The New York Times 2019

152   Talks at Google 2017

153   GXTalks 2019

154   GXTalks 2019

155   GXTalks 2019

156   Rise Conference 2018

157   Talks at Google 2017

158   Techjuice 2021

159   Standard Chartered 2019

160   The New York Times, 2008

161   The New York Times, 2008

162   APEC Summit 2012

163   The New York Times 2008

164   The New York Times 2008

165   Money.com 2015

166   Forbes 2011

167   APEC Summit 2012

168   Billboard Magazine 2021

169   APEC Summit 2012

170   The New York Times 2008

171   AEPC Summit 2013

172   IIT Delhi 2020

173   APEC Summit 2012

174   APEC Summit 2012

175   Computer Hope 2020

176   First International Computer 2020

177   AEPC Summit 2013

178   IIT Delhi 2020

179   AEPC Summit 2013

180   AEPC Summit 2013

181   IIT Delhi 2020

182   The New York Times 2008

183   Inc 2020

184   IIT Delhi 2020

185   IIT Delhi 2020

186   PhoneArea 2020

187   The Guardian 2019

188   Wired 2014

189   Quartz Africa 2019

190   Spero Ventures 2017

191   Forbes 2020

192   TechCrunch 2019

193   TechCrunch 2021

194   Medium 2016

195   Foursquare Church 2021

196   Faith Driven Investor 2021

197 TEDx 2019

198 TEDx 2019

199 TEDx 2019

200 TEDx 2019

201 Bella Naija 2011

202 Faith Driven Investor 2021

203 Faith Driven Investor 2021

204 Medium 2016

205 Medium 2016

206 Biztorials 2016

207 Village Capital Media 2017

208 Viktoria Ventures 2020

209 CoinDesk 2020

210 TechCrunch 2021

211 Crunchbase News 2021

212 China Highlights 2021

213 The Economist 2020

214 Bervell 2021

215 CNBCAfrica 2018

216 CNBCAfrica 2018

217 Business Elites Africa 2021

218 Biztorials TV 2016

219 Faith Driven Investor
     Podcast 2021

220 This Week in Startups
     2018

221 Biztorials TV 2016

222 Daxx 2020

223 Forbes 2020

224 Statista 2021

225 TechCrunch 2016

226 TechCrunch 2016

227 TechCrunch 2016

228 Spero Ventures 2017

229 This Week in Startups
     2018

230 This Week in Startups
     2018

231 Amazon Web Services
     2019

232 TEDx 2016

233 Catalyst 2007

234 Harvard Business Review
     2012

235 Spero Ventures 2017

236 Arise News 2018

237 Bloomberg Technology
     2016

238 Spero Ventures 2017

239 USA Today 2020

240 TechCrunch 2016

241 Brandcrunch 2021

242 Eden Life 2021

243 TEDx 2019

244 Viva Technology 2016

245 DMR, 2021

246 The New York Times 2006

247 Carl Hendy 2020

248 Taipei Times 2006

249 The New York Times 2006

250 The New York Times 2006

251 The Startups Team 2017

252 Empire Software Engi-
     neering 2017

253 Taipei Times 2006

254 RankDex 2020

255 Your Tech Story 2019

256 Lawrence Page 1997

257 Luxatic 2020

258 Taipei Times 2006

259 Taipei Times 2006

260 Taipei Times 2006

261 China Daily 2009

262 Taipei Times 2006

263 Lin 2009

264 Baidu 2020

265 Barboza 2006

266 Luxatic 2020

267 Stanford Technology
     Venture Program 2009

268 Barboza 2006

269 Barboza 2006

270 Lin 2009

271 Stanford Technology
     Ventures Program 2009

272 Stanford Technology
     Ventures Program 2009

273 Luxatic 2020

274 Stanford Technology
     Ventures Program 2009

275 China Daily 2009

276 Barboza 2006

277 Taipei Times 2006

278 The Economic Times 2020

279 The Economic Times 2020

280 Washington Business
     Journal 2019

281 Phocuswright 2019

282 OYO Blog 2020;/ Business
     Insider 2019

283 Accel 2019

284 VCC TV 2015

285 YourStory 2020

286 YourStory 2020

287 CNBC-TV18 2018

288 CNBC-TV18 2018

289 VCC TV 2015

290 VCC TV 2015

291 VCC TV 2015

292 Mint 2015

293 CNBC-TV18 2018

294 BML Munjal University
     2019

295 BML Munjal University
     2019

296 YourStory 2020

297 Harvard Business School
     2017

298 Nas Daily 2020

299 BML Munjal University
     2019

300 CNBC-TV18 2018

301 Inc42 2020

302 CNBC-TV18 2018

303 CNBC-TV18 2018

304 Inc42 2020

305   How to Start a Startup
2017

306   BML Munjal University
2019

307   The Asena Post 2019

308   South-Eastern Asia Population 2021

309   Reuters 2018

310   TechCrunch 2018

311   Forbes Asia 2015

312   Forbes Asia 2015

313   The Straits Times 2017

314   Bloomberg Technology
2019

315   The Straits Times 2017

316   The Straits Times 2017

317   The Straits Times 2017

318   Bloomberg Technology
2019

319   The Edge Markets 2018

320   Bloomberg Technology
2019

321   The Straits Times 2017

322   Nikkei Asia 2019

323   Bloomberg Technology
2019

324   Boston: American Inno
2011

325   Bloomberg Technology
2019

326   Goldman Sachs 2019

327   Goldman Sachs 2019

328   RISE Conference 2018

329   TechCrunch 2014

330   Born2Invest 2017

331   Bloomberg Technology
2019

332   Goldman Sachs 2019

333   Brand24 2015

334   Bloomberg Technology
2019

335   The New York Times 2013

336   RISE Conference, 2016

337   Nikkei Asia 2019

338   Nikkei Asia 2019

339   Goldman Sachs 2019

340   Goldman Sachs 2019

341   Goldman Sachs 2019

342   Rise Conference 2018

343   Berima 2019

344   Collins 1994

345   Music Business Worldwide 2019

346   Musically 2019

347   Bloomberg Businessweek
2017

348   Forbes 2019

349   Billboard 7

350   Katsiaficas 2012; Vox 2018

351   MBC Festival 2012

352   Waitt 2014

353   Vox 2018

354   Statista 2021

355   Brandwatch 2021

356 The Guardian 2020

357 New York Post 2018; South China Morning Post 2018

358 Fortune 2020

359 Showbiz CheatSheet 2020

360 Time 2019; Billboard 2019

361 Korea Now 2019

362 BangtanSubs 2019

363 BangtanSubs 2019

364 Joins News 2010

365 KPop Herald 2017

366 Join News 2010

367 Joonie Toon 2018

368 Join News 2010

369 Asian Entertainment and Culture 2020

370 SBS News 2011

371 Asian Entertainment and Culture 2020

372 Asian Entertainment and Culture, 2020

373 Sherylle Jeniffer 2020

374 Korea Now 2019

375 Statista 2021

376 Asian Entertainment and Culture 2020

377 Vanity Fair 2020

378 Asian Entertainment and Culture 2020

379 The Army Vlog 2017

380 BangtanSubs 2019

381 Brandwatch 2021

382 Asian Entertainment and Culture 2020

383 Vanity Fair, 2020

384 BangtanSubs 2019

385 Vanity Fair 2020

386 BangtanSubs 2019

387 Bervell 2020

388 Fortune 2021